FOUNDATIONAL CYBERSECURITY RESEARCH

IMPROVING SCIENCE, ENGINEERING, AND INSTITUTIONS

Lynette I. Millett, Baruch Fischhoff, Peter J. Weinberger, *Editors*

Computer Science and Telecommunications Board

Division on Engineering and Physical Sciences

A Consensus Study Report of

The National Academies of
SCIENCES · ENGINEERING · MEDICINE

THE NATIONAL ACADEMIES PRESS
Washington, DC
www.nap.edu

THE NATIONAL ACADEMIES PRESS   500 Fifth Street, NW   Washington, DC 20001

This project was supported by the National Security Agency with assistance from the National Science Foundation under award number CNS-1400278. Any opinions, findings, conclusions, or recommendations expressed in this publication do not necessarily reflect the views of any organization or agency that provided support for this project.

International Standard Book Number-13:   978-0-309-45529-9
International Standard Book Number-10:   0-309-45529-4
Digital Object Identifier: https://doi.org/10.17226/24676

Additional copies of this publication are available for sale from the National Academies Press, 500 Fifth Street, NW, Keck 360, Washington, DC 20001; (800) 624-6242 or (202) 334-3313; http://www.nap.edu.

Suggested citation: National Academies of Sciences, Engineering, and Medicine. 2017. *Foundational Cybersecurity Research: Improving Science, Engineering, and Institutions.* Washington, DC: The National Academies Press. https://doi.org/10.17226/24676.

The National Academies of
SCIENCES · ENGINEERING · MEDICINE

The **National Academy of Sciences** was established in 1863 by an Act of Congress, signed by President Lincoln, as a private, nongovernmental institution to advise the nation on issues related to science and technology. Members are elected by their peers for outstanding contributions to research. Dr. Marcia McNutt is president.

The **National Academy of Engineering** was established in 1964 under the charter of the National Academy of Sciences to bring the practices of engineering to advising the nation. Members are elected by their peers for extraordinary contributions to engineering. Dr. C. D. Mote, Jr., is president.

The **National Academy of Medicine** (formerly the Institute of Medicine) was established in 1970 under the charter of the National Academy of Sciences to advise the nation on medical and health issues. Members are elected by their peers for distinguished contributions to medicine and health. Dr. Victor J. Dzau is president.

The three Academies work together as the **National Academies of Sciences, Engineering, and Medicine** to provide independent, objective analysis and advice to the nation and conduct other activities to solve complex problems and inform public policy decisions. The National Academies also encourage education and research, recognize outstanding contributions to knowledge, and increase public understanding in matters of science, engineering, and medicine.

Learn more about the National Academies of Sciences, Engineering, and Medicine at **www.nationalacademies.org**.

The National Academies of
SCIENCES · ENGINEERING · MEDICINE

Consensus Study Reports published by the National Academies of Sciences, Engineering, and Medicine document the evidence-based consensus on the study's statement of task by an authoring committee of experts. Reports typically include findings, conclusions, and recommendations based on information gathered by the committee and the committee's deliberations. Each report has been subjected to a rigorous and independent peer-review process and it represents the position of the National Academies on the statement of task.

Proceedings published by the National Academies of Sciences, Engineering, and Medicine chronicle the presentations and discussions at a workshop, symposium, or other event convened by the National Academies. The statements and opinions contained in proceedings are those of the participants and are not endorsed by other participants, the planning committee, or the National Academies.

For information about other products and activities of the National Academies, please visit www.nationalacademies.org/about/whatwedo.

COMMITTEE ON FUTURE RESEARCH GOALS AND DIRECTIONS FOR FOUNDATIONAL SCIENCE IN CYBERSECURITY

BARUCH FISCHHOFF, Carnegie Mellon University, *Co-Chair*
PETER WEINBERGER, Google, Inc., *Co-Chair*
JANDRIA S. ALEXANDER, The Aerospace Corporation
ANNIE ANTÓN, Georgia Institute of Technology
STEVEN M. BELLOVIN, Columbia University
SEYMOUR E. GOODMAN, Georgia Institute of Technology
RONALD L. GRAHAM, University of California, San Diego
CARL E. LANDWEHR, Independent Consultant
STEVEN B. LIPNER, SAFECode
ROY A. MAXION, Carnegie Mellon University
GREG MORRISETT, Cornell University
BRIAN SNOW, Independent Consultant
PHIL VENABLES, Goldman Sachs
STEVEN J. WALLACH, Micron Technology

Staff

LYNETTE I. MILLETT, Associate Director and Senior Program Officer
VIRGINIA BACON TALATI, Program Officer

Preface

This study emerged from an informal request to the National Academies of Sciences, Engineering, and Medicine's Computer Science and Telecommunications Board (CSTB) from Brad Martin of the National Security Agency. The project was initiated by the Special Cyber Operations Research and Engineering (SCORE) Interagency Working Group and sponsored with assistance from the National Science Foundation. The statement of task for the Committee on Future Research Goals and Directions for Foundational Science in Cybersecurity, established by the National Academies to carry out this study, is as follows:

> An ad hoc National Research Council committee will conduct a multi-phased sequential study to consider future research goals and directions for foundational science in cybersecurity, to include relevant efforts in economics and behavioral science as well as more "traditional" cybersecurity topics. It will also consider how investments in foundational work support mission needs in the long term. The committee will review current unclassified and classified cybersecurity research strategies, plans, and programs as well as requirements in both domains. It will consider major challenge problems, explore proposed new directions, identify gaps in the current portfolio, consider the complementary roles of research in unclassified and classified settings, and consider how foundational work in an unclassified setting can be translated to meet national security objectives. Phase 1 will involve preliminary data gathering and analysis by the committee, but no report will be issued. In Phase 2, the committee will undertake additional data gathering, analysis, and deliberations. In Phase 3, the committee would extend

its data gathering and analysis from Phase 2. The study will result in two reports: (1) a public report at the conclusion of Phase 2 providing a high-level roadmap for foundational cybersecurity research based only on public domain information and (2) an additional, brief public report and a non-public classified annex as necessary reflecting the committee's work in Phase 3.

This report is the result of Phase 2. The committee, whose biographies are listed in Appendix B, gathered input through a number of data-gathering sessions. The committee appreciates the insights and perspectives provided by the experts who presented briefings; they are listed in Appendix A.

With a perennial societal challenge like cybersecurity, a topic that has been explored extensively and where real breakthroughs have proven elusive, a challenge is to avoid well-trodden ground. The committee was mindful of the sponsor's request to focus on opportunities where a fresh approach to the problem could prove fruitful. Thus, this report does not present a list of hard open research problems (there are many such worthy lists, some of which are summarized in Appendix C) nor argue for specific programs. Instead, the committee offers alternative approaches to framing research problems, organizing research programs, and integrating research and practice. We hope to offer fresh ways to realize the potential of the resources and intellect invested in addressing cybersecurity challenges.

This report represents the cooperative effort of many people. We thank the individuals who came to speak with us during the course of the study. We appreciate the work of our committee. Circumstances beyond the committee's control delayed activity at certain phases of the project, and we appreciate its members' patience and that of our sponsors throughout the process. We also thank the reviewers whose comments helped to strengthen the report considerably.

Baruch Fischhoff and Peter Weinberger, *Co-Chairs*
Committee on Future Research Goals and Directions
for Foundational Science in Cybersecurity

Acknowledgment of Reviewers

This Consensus Study Report was reviewed in draft form by individuals chosen for their diverse perspectives and technical expertise. The purpose of this independent review is to provide candid and critical comments that will assist the National Academies of Sciences, Engineering, and Medicine in making each published report as sound as possible and to ensure that it meets the institutional standards for quality, objectivity, evidence, and responsiveness to the study charge. The review comments and draft manuscript remain confidential to protect the integrity of the deliberative process.

We thank the following individuals for their review of this report:

Robert Axelrod, University of Michigan,
Frederick Chang, Southern Methodist University,
John McLean, Naval Research Laboratory,
Peter Neumann, SRI International,
Robert Oliver, University of California, Berkeley,
Shari Lawrence Pfleeger, Dartmouth College,
Angela Sasse, University College London,
William Scherlis, Carnegie Mellon University, and
Fred Schneider, Cornell University.

Although the reviewers listed above provided many constructive comments and suggestions, they were not asked to endorse the conclusions or recommendations of this report nor did they see the final draft before its release. The review of this report was overseen by William H. Press, University of Texas, Austin. He was responsible for making certain that an independent examination of this report was carried out in accordance with the standards of the National Academies and that all review comments were carefully considered. Responsibility for the final content rests entirely with the authoring committee and the National Academies.

Contents

APPENDIXES

Summary

Attaining meaningful cybersecurity presents a broad societal challenge. Its complexity and the range of systems and sectors in which it is needed mean that successful approaches are necessarily multifaceted. Moreover, cybersecurity is a dynamic process involving human attackers who continue to adapt. Despite considerable investments of resources and intellect, cybersecurity continues to pose serious challenges to national security, business performance, and public well-being. Modern developments in computation, storage, and connectivity to the Internet have brought into even sharper focus the need for a better understanding of the overall security of the systems we depend on.

The research cultures that have developed in the security community and in affiliated disciplines will increasingly need to incorporate lessons not just from a wider variety of disciplines, but also from practitioners, developers, and system administrators responsible for securing real-world operational systems. This report is aimed primarily at the cybersecurity research community, but takes a broad view that efforts to improve foundational cybersecurity research will need to include many disciplines working together to achieve common goals.

There have been many reports on cybersecurity research offering many recommendations. Rather than echo these reports and expand their lists of proposed projects, the committee has focused on foundational research *strategies* for organizing people, technologies, and governance. These strategies seek to ensure the sustained support needed to create an agile, effective research community, with collaborative links across disciplines and between research and practice.

Part of the task of the Committee on Future Research Goals and Directions for Foundational Science in Cybersecurity was to consider gaps in the federal research program. In the committee's view, the security community and funders understand the breadth of the challenge and the importance of emphasizing progress on all fronts—a diversity evident in the diverse approaches taken by the federal agencies supporting cybersecurity research. Instead of focusing on gaps, this report offers a framework that links research efforts. The strategy advocated below requires unusual collaborations among disciplines focused on technologies and those focused on the individuals and organizations that try to attack and protect them. Achieving those collaborations will require creating incentives that run counter to academic pressure for publications and user pressures for short-term results.

To this end, the committee's analysis is organized under the four following broad aims for cybersecurity research:

- *Support, develop, and improve security science*—a long-term, inclusive, multidisciplinary approach to security science.
- *Integrate the social, behavioral, and decision sciences into the security science research effort*, since all cybersecurity challenges and mitigations involve people and organizations.
- *Integrate engineering and operations* for a life-cycle understanding of systems.
- *Sustain long-term support for security science research* providing institutional and community opportunities to support these approaches.

Not every research effort will or needs to address all four aims. However, articulating where each sits with respect to them is important to the coherence of the research program. These four aims are discussed below.

STRENGTHEN THE SCIENTIFIC
UNDERPINNINGS OF CYBERSECURITY

Security science has the goal of improving understanding of which aspects of a system (including its environment and users) create vulnerabilities or enable someone or something (inside or outside the system) to exploit them. Ideally, security science provides not just predictions for when attacks are likely to succeed, but also evidence linking cause and effect pointing to solution mechanisms. A science of security would develop over time, for example, a body of scientific laws, testable explanations, predictions about systems, and confirmation or validation of predicted outcomes.

A scientific approach to cybersecurity challenges could enrich understanding of the existing landscape of systems, defenses, attacks, and adversaries. Clear and well-substantiated models could help identify potential payoffs and support of mission needs while avoiding likely dead ends and poor places to invest effort. There are strong and well-developed bases in the contributing disciplines. In mathematics and computer science, these include work in logic, computational complexity, and game theory. In the human sciences, they include work in judgment, decision making, interface design, and organizational behavior.

INCLUDE THE SOCIAL, BEHAVIORAL, AND DECISION SCIENCES IN SECURITY SCIENCE

Technical approaches alone will not suffice for cybersecurity as long as humans play roles in systems as developers, users, operators, or adversaries. Major security breakdowns have occurred because individuals misplace trust, organizations create perverse incentives, or adversaries discover and exploit design flaws. Meeting security needs effectively requires understanding that human context. How does cybersecurity affect the real-world business or organization? Does it drain human or other resources, or does it reflect a balance between keeping the business or organization secure and keeping it economically viable? What investments does it deserve and receive? How does the perceived value of possible practices compare with their demonstrated efficacy? What evidence would help to make that assessment? Social, behavioral, and decision sciences provide the reservoir of knowledge for addressing some of these questions and for making other research more useful for those responsible for vulnerable systems. Such expertise can also be vital, especially during design, for revealing any disconnects between intention and actual use and in articulating the variety of potential users and their contexts.

Human behavior affects all stages of the life cycle of a cybersecurity system: design, implementation, operation, maintenance, monitoring, revision, and replacement. Each stage offers opportunities to increase or reduce vulnerability: how design teams are constituted and managed, how procedures and interfaces are tested for usability, what incentives and resources are provided for security, how operators are trained and their performance evaluated, how the business case is made and understood. Our adversaries' systems have their own life cycles, which might be disrupted at each stage. As a result, achieving effective cybersecurity will depend on understanding and addressing human dimensions of systems. Doing so will require overcoming psychological and institutional impediments that make effective collaboration difficult.

On the whole, the traditional cybersecurity community lacks expertise in social science analysis tools and methods. As a result, it not only relies on intuition, when it could draw on science available, but also struggles in its attempts to validate its approaches, falling below scientific standards in experimental design. Collaborating with social scientists and understanding their standards for research and publication would bring new tools to bear and yield new insights. A psychological barrier to such collaborations is that system designers and operators have unwarranted confidence in their intuitive theories about others' behavior. Indeed, the human–computer interaction research community has a motto, "You are not the user," to remind researchers and practitioners not to assume that other people share their perceptions and motivations.

The primary institutional barrier to utilizing the social, behavioral, and decision science expertise is that these disciplines are largely absent from the cybersecurity research community. Indeed, the community often lacks even the absorptive capacity to identify these needs, recruit the expertise needed to address them, and critically evaluate claims about system security elements that can be compromised by human failures in design, deployment, training, or management. Without that expertise, the cybersecurity community must improvise its own theories and research methods that are central to those sciences: experimental design, identifying confounds, meta-analysis, sensitivity analysis, and so on. Conversely, because those sciences have not been drawn into addressing the unique challenges of cybersecurity, they have limited experience in applying (and explaining) their research to those domains and in identifying the unique foundational research questions that they pose.

To create more effective collaborations, it is essential to foster interactions that address the needs of both these disciplines and the cybersecurity community. One thing cross-disciplinary researchers can do is to evaluate how well a result from one context will hold true in another.

The committee identifies barriers to collaboration both within and among the disciplines and discusses strategic institutional options to overcome them. Those strategies include creating institutional settings with the following: support reserved for projects that are jointly defined by members of different disciplines; working groups with the sustained interpersonal contact needed to create trusted relationships and absorb one another's work practices; training programs in the essentials of other disciplines, both short term for working professionals and extended at the undergraduate, graduate, and postdoctoral levels; and positions that require their holders to demonstrate both practical and academic accomplishments.

Cybersecurity poses grand challenges that require unique collaborations among the best people in the relevant core disciplines, who typically have other options for their time and energy. Sponsors of cybersecurity research need to create the conditions that make it worth their while to work on these issues. If successful, cybersecurity research will benefit not only from the substantive knowledge of the social, behavioral, and decision sciences, but also from absorbing their research culture with respect to theory building, hypothesis testing, method validation, experimentation, and knowledge accumulation—just as they will learn from the complementary expertise of the cybersecurity community. Thus, these collaborations have transformative potential for the participating disciplines, while addressing the urgent practical problems of cybersecurity.

ADDRESS ENGINEERING, OPERATIONAL, AND LIFE-CYCLE CHALLENGES IN SECURITY SCIENCE

Improving cybersecurity requires that security considerations be integrated into the practice of hardware and software development and deployment. Research in many key technical areas can embed assumptions about, for example, agility and expected operations and maintenance, or research can be focused on how to improve post-deployment activities related to systems. That is, research that focuses on how maintenance and system administration affect overall system performance is part of a holistic approach to cybersecurity research.

In this spirit, software development organizations developing commodity systems have made substantial efforts to improve their practices and systems. These organizations have, over time, created development practices for reducing the prevalence of exploitable vulnerabilities in released software. A critical component of these approaches is feedback loops tracing discovered vulnerabilities or attacks to root causes. Applied systematically, these feedback loops can lead to new tools or techniques and are fundamental to improving cybersecurity. These efforts are an essential part of security science, integrating what is known about state-of-the-art software engineering practices; social, behavioral, and organizational theory; current understandings of the threat landscape; and models of attacks and defenses. Practical lessons from companies working at the cutting edge of secure system development can inform research approaches that incorporate scientific models.

System administrators and other practitioners are often on the frontlines of securing systems. It is important to develop mechanisms whereby researchers can learn about the real problems being experienced in the field by practitioners. Opportunities include work on resilient architectures, composition of components and properties, logging systems, variability, and configuration. Researchers in these areas benefit significantly from industry contacts and trust relationships with practitioner colleagues.

Research is also needed on metrics useful for informing organizational practices. As a starting point, the measures practiced by the most successful organizations could be made public in a way that makes them available for use as metrics by others. This work would need to be kept up-to-date. Research on what can be done in terms of organizational practices and the extent to which practices enhance security is needed. Adversaries change tactics and approaches frequently, and the organizations that hope to defend themselves must adapt continuously. Security science here will involve understanding how science, models, attacks, and defenses interact; how systems are engineered, deployed, and maintained; and how organizations decide to invest in, develop, and promulgate technologies, practices, and policies regarding security.

The traditional decoupling of academic research from engineering, quality control, and operations leaves gaps in a domain like cybersecurity, where solutions are needed for systems deployed at scale in the real world. These gaps highlight the importance of not just technology transfer, but of incorporating a life-cycle perspective (from development to deployment, maintenance, administration, and aftermarket activities) into proposed foundational research approaches.

SUPPORT AND SUSTAIN FOUNDATIONAL
RESEARCH FOR SECURITY SCIENCE

This report is intended to complement the federal Networking and Information Technology Research and Development Program's 2016 *Federal Cybersecurity Research and Development Strategic Plan*.[1] It elaborates on several specific components of the strategic plan and offers a framework for organizing that research. Most elements of the research agenda in this report can be mapped to components of the strategic plan. The committee outlines a foundational technical research agenda clustered around three broad themes that correspond to those in the strategic plan: detect (detection and attribution of attacks and vulnerabilities), protect (defensible systems that are prepared for and can resist attacks), and adapt (resilient systems that can recover from or cope with a wide range of adversarial behavior). Many familiar technical topics fall within these clusters. Many challenges span them—making an understanding of how they interact critical.

Research that links social, behavioral, and decision sciences and cybersecurity should encourage advances in cybersecurity practices

---

[1] National Science and Technology Council, *Federal Cybersecurity Research and Development Strategic Plan: Ensuring Prosperity and National Security*, Networking and Information Technology Research and Development Program, February 2016.

and outcomes. Illustrative topics include the following: how individuals interact with and mentally model systems, risk, and vulnerability; incentives and practices in organizations; adversary assessment; why and how cybersecurity measures are adopted; and managing conflicting needs and values in policy, organizations, and technologies. A better understanding of how policies, practices, and improvements are adopted (or neglected) would allow organizational science to leverage cybersecurity research. Two overarching research challenges are how to assess the criticality of a particular capability or application in a given context and how to evaluate the results of research and prioritize implementation. In both cases, there are opportunities to apply foundational science to cybersecurity needs.

FOSTER INSTITUTIONAL APPROACHES AND OPPORTUNITIES TO IMPROVE SECURITY SCIENCE

The research cultures that have developed in the security community and affiliated disciplines will increasingly need to adjust to embrace and incorporate lessons from both a wider variety of disciplines and practitioners, including the developers, and administrators responsible for securing real-world operational systems. Given the dynamic, rapidly evolving nature of the problem, the cybersecurity research community itself has struggled to develop a sustained science of security. A 2016 Computing Research Association (CRA) memo[2] suggests that computing research suffers from counterproductive incentives emphasizing publication quantity and short-term results, inhibiting longer-term efforts and infrastructure development. This report proposes strategies to address these counterproductive incentives.

The committee was asked to consider gaps in the federal research program. In the committee's view, the security community and funders understand the breadth of the challenge. The gaps that the committee identified are not strictly topics or problems that are not being addressed. Instead, the committee focused on how programs and projects are framed and conducted, with an emphasis on creating integrative security science that is capable of seeking and incorporating relevant social, behavioral, and decision science results and operational and life-cycle understandings.

The committee was also asked to consider how foundational efforts in cybersecurity bear on mission-critical applications and challenges, such as those faced by agencies working in classified domains. From the commit-

---

[2] B. Friedman and F.B. Schneider, "Incentivizing Quality and Impact: Evaluating Scholarship in Hiring, Tenure, and Promotion," 2015, *Computing Research Association*, http://cra.org/resources/best-practice-memos/incentivizing-quality-and-impact-evaluating-scholarship-in-hiring-tenure-and-promotion/.

tee's perspective, the same principles apply, whatever the domains (from protecting systems that contain information on an intelligence agency's sources and methods, to preventing the servers running the latest best-selling augmented reality mobile game from being compromised, to general deterrence efforts).

Thus, foundational efforts in cybersecurity, as described in this report, could yield results that are broadly applicable. One potential distinction the committee considered was between classified and unclassified efforts: Although there may be differences in the nature of threat and what is known and by whom about that threat, private-sector entities are increasingly on the front line, facing and securing themselves against "nation-state"-level attacks. Moreover, even if people and processes differ in public- and private-sector organizations, all depend on human behavior of the sort that social, behavioral, and decision science research integrated with technical cybersecurity research can inform.

There are also research efforts in the classified and unclassified domains that leverage similarities in basic technologies, humans interacting with systems, and organizations managing them. Making those connections is not always done, however. It falls to funders, the researchers, and the consumers of research to make those connections. Problems and assumptions may need to be translated across the classified/unclassified boundary, but foundational results should be applicable in each. It will be particularly important to develop and find people who are skilled at these translations.

* * *

The challenge of cybersecurity and the urgent nature of risks to society posed by insecure systems and a dynamic and fast-changing environment understandably promotes an emphasis on moving fast. Paradoxically, however, the field is still so comparatively new, and the nature of the challenge is so hard, that in-depth scientific research is needed to understand the very nature of the artifacts in use, the nature of software, the complexity and interdependencies in these human-built systems, and importantly, how the humans and organizations who design, build, use, and attack the systems affect what can be known and understood about them. Encouraging research to address these challenges will require sustained commitments and engagements. Thus, programs that encourage long-horizon projects where these connections can be worked out will be important.

The fact that these systems are designed, developed, deployed, and used by humans, and that humans are also the adversaries behind attacks on them, means that the work done in the social, behavioral, and decision sciences will be critical. Deepening understanding of humans and human organizations, and linking that understanding to more traditional research in cybersecurity, is necessary to develop a robust security science and to deploy systems most effectively so that they do what they were designed to do, secured against human adversaries. Cybersecurity can be viewed as a cutting edge of computing that demands a broad, multidisciplinary effort. Addressing the global cybersecurity challenge needs not just computer science, engineering science, and mathematics, but also partnerships with other disciplines to draw on what we know and understand about human nature and how humans interact with and manage systems—and each other.

1

Cybersecurity Challenges and Security Science

Despite considerable investments of resources and intellect, cybersecurity continues to pose serious challenges to national security, business performance, and public well-being. Modern developments in computation, storage, and connectivity to the Internet have brought into even sharper focus the need for a better understanding of the overall security of the systems we depend on.

The cybersecurity task is daunting, and the world continues to change. We see increasing replacement of physical systems with digital ones, increasing use of digital systems by larger segments of the population, and increasing use of digital systems in ways that the designers and developers never intended. In the early days, the security focus was on protecting networks, servers, and client workstations. Today's concerns include targeted attacks on electromechanical control systems and mobile devices. Systems of all kinds are becoming larger and more interconnected. Other changes in recent years include the character of the threat, its sophistication, goals and targets; increasingly sophisticated supply chains for software-reliant systems that themselves include components from diverse sources; and wide deployment of Internet of Things (IoT) devices (e.g., infrastructure controlled by SCADA systems,[1] home automation, and self-driving and partly automated vehicles and automated highways). Success in protecting one area drives attackers to probe

---

[1] SCADA refers to Supervisory Control and Data Acquisition systems typically used to monitor and control industrial processes in the physical world.

elsewhere. All of these trends result in larger impacts when systems are compromised.

This committee was asked to consider future research goals and directions for foundational science in cybersecurity, including economics and behavioral science as well as more "traditional" cybersecurity topics. It brought together researchers from different disciplines and practitioners from different sectors.

There have been many reports on cybersecurity research offering many recommendations. Rather than echo those reports and expand their lists of proposed projects, the committee focused on foundational research *strategies* for organizing people, technologies, and governance. These strategies seek to ensure the sustained support needed to create an agile and effective research community, with collaborative links across disciplines and between research and practice. The aim of the report is to encompass a broad *security science* that includes fundamental underpinnings related to scientific laws, attacks, policies, and environments;[2] social, behavioral, and decision science considerations; as well as engineering, operational, and life-cycle challenges. This report is aimed primarily at the cybersecurity research community, but it takes a broad view that efforts to improve foundational science in cybersecurity will need to be inclusive of many disciplinary perspectives and ensure that these disciplines work together to achieve common goals.[3]

CHALLENGES TO ACHIEVING CYBERSECURITY

Cyberspace is notoriously vulnerable to varied and changing attacks by hackers, criminals, terrorists, and state actors. The nation's critical infrastructure, including the electric power grid, air traffic control system, financial system, and communication networks, depends on information technology for its operation and thus is susceptible to cyberattack. These concerns are not new, nor is recognition of the importance of research as an essential element in U.S. national cybersecurity strategy. For example, as early as 1991, the National Academies of Sciences, Engineering, and Medicine highlighted the role of research in understanding and address-

---

[2] This formulation was first described in F.B. Schneider, Blueprint for a science of cybersecurity, *The Next Wave* 19(2), 2012.

[3] Regarding privacy: Although the committee was tasked to consider cybersecurity, there is overlap in the cybersecurity and privacy research communities (and research problems). And privacy research itself demands input from many disciplines. As an end, protecting privacy is one measure of system performance. As a means, compromised privacy can create openings for other mischief; fear over compromise may motivate behavior that benefits the system overall. Many of the approaches suggested in this report should also apply to privacy research, even if the particular examples do not overlap directly.

ing vulnerabilities through scientifically sound policies, technologies, and behavioral interventions.[4] It focused on end-to-end strategies, linking the previously stovepiped domains of communications security and system security. The present report adopts the same encompassing view.

Why is the cybersecurity situation so challenging despite years of attention? One major challenge is that we rely on systems and components that were not designed with modern threats in mind. Many of these systems and components are intrinsically weak due to decades-old design choices as well as outdated security goals and assumptions about the nature of the threat. Another challenge is that even well-designed systems have bugs, creating vulnerabilities that attackers will work hard to find—and often succeed in finding. Many systems evolve over time, combining newer components with legacy components; often this evolution occurs with only limited application of systems engineering principles and without an understanding of what the security-critical components are or the dependencies on them.

Despite growing awareness of these threats, many organizations still do not (or cannot) spend the resources needed to understand or fix their vulnerabilities. When they see software as safety-critical, other concerns (e.g., costs, schedules) may limit their efforts to improve systems security. Moreover, fallible humans design, maintain, use, and repair systems in ways that may unintentionally expose and facilitate ease of break-in. This report bears these realities in mind, considering the behavioral and organizational interventions needed to sustain improvements needed for more securely designed, more bug-free, and more error-tolerant systems at acceptable cost.

Another difficulty is that many actors affect cybersecurity, including boards of directors, shareholders, regulators, standards bodies, citizens, nongovernmental organizations, manufacturers, and researchers. As a result, there are often conflicting views and interests. For instance, password requirements for online banking tend to be much less strict than those used inside the federal government, reflecting different trade-offs. At a societal level, cybersecurity affects and is affected by the sometimes conflicting equities of national security, democratic values, and economic prosperity,[5] which widens the aperture for the research enterprise considerably.

Responding to these dynamic challenges requires sustained support for research that can address challenges of today and those still on the horizon.

---

[4] National Research Council, *Computers at Risk: Safe Computing in the Information Age*, National Academy Press, Washington, D.C., 1991.

[5] See "Tensions Between Cybersecurity and Other Public Policy Concerns," Chapter 7 in National Research Council, *At the Nexus of Cybersecurity and Public Policy: Some Basic Concepts and Issues*, The National Academies Press, Washington, D.C., 2014.

It requires collaboration across disciplines, because overall system security depends on individual and organizational behavior as well as technology. It requires the ability to reconfigure approaches as threats (and successes) evolve, which means having short cycles for receiving and responding to feedback. Meeting these requirements will not be easy in a world organized around scientific disciplines, corporations and institutions, regulatory and standards bodies, and government bureaucracies—each functioning in ways that have been developed in the past to focus on other areas. For these reasons, the committee has primarily focused on processes for identifying and addressing problems, rather than on problems per se.

SCIENTIFIC UNDERPINNINGS OF CYBERSECURITY

Security science[6] has the goal of improving the understanding of which aspects of a system (including its environment and users) create vulnerabilities or enable someone or something (inside or outside the system) to exploit them. Ideally, security science provides not just predictions for when attacks are likely to succeed, but also evidence linking cause and effect pointing to solution mechanisms. A science of security would develop over time, for example, a body of scientific laws, testable explanations, predictions about systems, and confirmation or validation of predicted outcomes.

As an example, adversaries discovered a new interface in an incomplete initial model and used side-channel attacks[7] to exploit it. A systematic, scientific approach to modeling the cryptographic system that took this into account allowed the model to be improved. Another example involves the common attack mode of "phishing," which is not against a technical system per se but against an individual, where an adversary tries to deceive someone into actions that allow attackers into their system. A model that does not include people invoking malicious software would be

---

[6] Recent years have seen increased discussion of what a scientific basis for cybersecurity might entail, and efforts are under way within the cybersecurity research community to develop a security science. See, for instance, F.B. Schneider, Blueprint for a science of cybersecurity, *The Next Wave* 19(2), 2012. Continued work in this space is a key component of the foundational approach described in this report. See also C. Herley and P. van Oorschot, "SoK: Science, Security, and the Elusive Science of Security," *Proceedings of 2017 IEEE Symposium on Security and Privacy* (forthcoming, available at http://people.scs.carleton.ca/~paulv/papers/oakland2017science.pdf). Building this science will be a long-term endeavor that is both forward-looking, in that its results can be used as a basis for decisions about current and future systems, and retrospective, in that results can be used to explain how and why past efforts failed (or succeeded). As more is understood, scientific analyses can be used to assess both proposed efforts and past practices.

[7] *Side-channel attacks* use information derived from the physical characteristics of a system (such as power consumption or electromagnetic leaks) to attack cryptographic systems, rather than exploiting algorithmic weaknesses, such as differential power analysis.

incomplete with respect to this type of attack, however complete it was in other respects. As long as their limits are known, scientific laws derived from incomplete models may still be useful. A set of mathematical laws about cryptography that addresses the strength of algorithms but not side-channel attacks could still help in designing systems that resist some attacks, even if not all kinds of adversaries.

A scientific approach to cybersecurity challenges could enrich understanding of the existing landscape of systems, defenses, attacks, and adversaries. Clear and well-substantiated models could help identify potential payoffs and support of mission needs while avoiding likely dead ends and poor places to invest effort. There are strong and well-developed bases in the contributing disciplines. In mathematics and computer science, these include work in logic, computational complexity, and game theory. In the human sciences, they include work in judgment, decision making, interface design, and organizational behavior.

EXAMPLE EFFORTS

Examples of research areas in which this sort of scientific approach has been taken include cryptography, programming languages, and security modeling. The cryptography community (which comes from a mathematics tradition) has taken a mathematical approach to problems related to secrecy, integrity, authentication, and non-repudiation. For example, researchers in this community developed approaches to probabilistic computational secrecy, cryptographic protocol analysis, and logics of authentication with mathematical models that allow the exploration of what is and is not possible with clearly stated assumptions. The cryptography community has developed a set of building blocks and constructive reasoning principles that allow building new approaches (e.g., protocols) whose security attributes can be estimated relative to known building blocks.

The programming language and semantics community has followed suit. One example is the work on type-based information flow, which now allows constructing models of languages or systems, and proving relevant properties (e.g., non-interference) and deriving implementations.[8] Another example is a proof that type checking and program obfuscation are equivalently effective against certain classes of attacks.[9] The security

---

[8] D.E. Denning and P.J. Denning, Certification of programs for secure information flow, *Communications of the ACM* 20(7):504-513, 1977; L. Zheng and A.C. Myers, "Dynamic Security Labels and Noninterference," Cornell University, https://www.cs.cornell.edu/andru/papers/dynl-tr.pdf.

[9] R. Pucella and F.B. Schneider, Independence from obfuscation: A semantic framework for diversity, *Journal of Computer Security* 18:701-749.

modeling community has formulated models of security since the 1970s,[10] as well as methods for evaluating these models.[11] This work was an instance where the science of security was advanced by introducing tools from another discipline (logic) to evaluate an accepted model.

Another example of research using a scientific approach considers abstract security mechanisms and what can be learned about their properties and applicability to classes of attacks. In the case of reference monitors—components of a system that allow certain things to happen (or not) based on a security policy—one interesting result is that firewalls, operating system kernels, and mechanisms that enforce access control lists are all reference monitors. Viewed from security science seeking general principle, researchers asked, What general security policies can a reference monitor enforce? The result is that reference monitors can enforce only what are known as safety properties, which require that something bad will never happen.[12] This result both demonstrates the robustness of the scientific approach and offers a practical insight to those implementing security technologies—to wit: understand whether the policy to be enforced is a safety property, and recognize that, if it is not, any security approach that depends on a reference monitor will not be able to enforce it. For instance, firewalls cannot address sophisticated phishing attacks.[13]

Developing scientific laws and models related to composability would help explore and explain how combinations of mechanisms and approaches interact.[14] It could be a key contribution, especially if exploring compos-

---

[10] D.E. Bell and L.J. LaPadula, "Secure Computer System: Unified Exposition and Multics Interpretation," MTR-2997, MITRE Corp., Bedford, Mass., March 1976, available as NTIS AD A023 588; J.A. Goguen and J. Meseguer, "Security Policies and Security Models," pp. 11-20 in *1982 IEEE Symposium on Security and Privacy*, 1982, http://ieeexplore.ieee.org/xpl/mostRecentIssue.jsp?punumber=6234453.

[11] J. McLean, "Reasoning about Security Models," *1987 IEEE Symposium on Security and Privacy*, IEEE, 1987, http://ieeexplore.ieee.org/xpl/mostRecentIssue.jsp?punumber=6234872.

[12] F.B. Schneider, Enforceable security policies, *ACM Transactions on Information and System Security* 3(1):30-50, 2000; K.W. Hamlen, G. Morrisett, and F.B. Schneider, Computability classes for enforcement mechanisms, *ACM Transactions on Programming Languages and Systems (TOPLAS)* 28(1):175-205, 2006.

[13] A given firewall may be able to institute a policy that would reject some set of phishing attacks but cannot defend against the entire class of phishing attacks—not least because a precise definition of "phishing" is not available. To correctly identify all phishing attacks would require a reference monitor that could understand natural language as well as being able to predict how a program would execute when it is downloaded. This suggests the need for research on a broader notion of phishing that relates to the structure of decision making in organizations and would draw on social, behavioral, and decision sciences, as discussed in Chapter 3.

[14] Some work has already been done in this area as well going at least as far back as J. McLean, A general theory of composition for a class of "possibilistic" properties, *IEEE Transactions on Software Engineering* 22(1):53-67, 1996.

ability mechanisms and approaches generates new knowledge about independence and its relationship to security. Results from that exploration could contribute significantly to the design and deployment of defensible systems. Reasoning about and understanding of the security of systems that have been synthesized from individual components or subsystems remains a challenging problem that is today best tackled by experts with expertise in attackers' techniques. Such experts are in short supply. Providing these experts with well-protected building blocks could help them work more effectively and efficiently toward a network-wide security approach as they focus on the seams between components (which are increasingly a target of adversaries). This would be particularly effective if those blocks can be verified or proved correct, together with a way to understand and model how they work together. Human factors researchers have developed signal detection theory[15] to determine when performance errors reflect the inability to detect problems and misaligned incentives for responding to them (undue or insufficient caution). They have developed vigilance theory[16] to predict the effects of work conditions (e.g., shift length) on performance. One series of studies combined the two in investigating susceptibility to phishing attacks, finding wide variability in both detection ability and perceived incentives across individuals, as well as differences within individuals when thinking about a potential threat and deciding how to respond. These resulting performance parameter estimates provide a basis for evaluating the relative vulnerability of alternative system configurations.[17]

Other questions inviting a scientific approach include the following:

- What are useful or "interesting" classes of attacks, defenses, and policies?
- What does it mean for systems or subsystems to be independent? Replication tolerates failures (because we believe physically separated devices fail independently), but replication does not tolerate attacks (because replicas have the same vulnerabilities). Defense in depth works when the component defenses are "independent."
- What are good underlying formalisms for execution? The formal methods community uses "sets of sequences," but this is too inexpressive for even simple security policies like confidentiality.

---

[15] S.K. Lynn and L.F. Barrett, "Utilizing" signal detection theory, *Psychological Science* 25(9):1663-1673, 2014, doi:10.1177/0956797614541991.

[16] N.H. Mackworth, The breakdown of vigilance during prolonged visual search, *Quarterly Journal of Experimental Psychology* 1(1):6-21, 1948, doi:10.1080/17470214808416738.

[17] C. Canfield, B. Fischhoff, and A.L. Davis, Quantifying phishing susceptibility for detection and behavior decisions, *Human Factors* 58(8):1158-1172, 2016, doi: 10.1177/0018720816665025.

- Is there an orthogonal set of building blocks related to security? Is there a natural correspondence between those building blocks and specific classes or mechanisms? The traditional security notions of confidentiality, integrity, and availability are intuitive, but they are not orthogonal, which complicates reasoning and analysis. (Confidentiality can be achieved by corrupting integrity or by denying access.)

Programmatically, there have been several efforts toward a science of security in the cybersecurity community, beginning in earnest a few years ago. As one example, the National Security Agency (NSA) has funded several lablets (groups of researchers tasked with contributing to the development of a systemic body of knowledge)[18] and created an annual "Best Scientific Cybersecurity Paper" competition.[19] As an adjunct to these lablets and related efforts, the NSA has also established a science of security virtual organization[20] to help researchers stay abreast of current news and activities in the field. There are currently four academic research lablets; they were established to focus on developing a science of security and a community to advance it. The lablets have developed lists of hard problems that involve crossing disciplinary boundaries, and the NSA has worked to get researchers to report results in relation to those problems.

The lablet model is designed to promote more direct interactions among researchers (i.e., not just through the literature) with a focus on sharing those diverse research methods that cybersecurity challenges require, including observational empiricism and data analysis, interventional empiricism, mathematical models, and reasoning. A science of security can lead to powerful and explanatory results and predictions. Drawing the connections between traditional cybersecurity research and emerging scientific laws and models, and making clear how such results fit within an overarching (albeit still emerging) science, will serve to both validate the science as it is developed and contextualize specific results.

OUTLINE OF THIS REPORT

The committee's analysis and recommendations in the rest of this report are organized under the four following broad aims:

---

[18] K. Dey, "NSA's Science of Security and Privacy Research Network Map," *Cyber-Physical Systems Virtual Organization*, 2016, http://cps-vo.org/group/sos/map.

[19] For more, see Cyber-Physical Systems Virtual Organization, "5th Annual Best Scientific Cybersecurity Paper Competition," http://cps-vo.org/group/sos/papercompetition, accessed September 2016.

[20] Cyber-Physical Systems Virtual Organization, "Science of Security VO: About," http://cps-vo.org/group/SoS/about, accessed September 2016.

- *Support, develop, and improve security science*—in terms of the emerging research efforts in this area, in the practice and reporting of results, and in terms of a long-term, inclusive, multidisciplinary approach to security science.
- *Integrate the social, behavioral, and decision sciences into the security science research effort*, since all cybersecurity challenges and mitigations involve people and organizations.
- *Integrate engineering and operations*, incorporating a life-cycle understanding of systems into the research endeavor and security science.
- *Sustain long-term support for security science research* including material resources and institutional structures that facilitate approaches and opportunities for improvement.

Box 1.1 illustrates these commitments in the context of the study of passwords. Although not every research effort in cybersecurity can

---

BOX 1.1
The Study of Passwords as an Authentication Tool

Authentication is a long-standing challenge for system design and engineering. Passwords have been used for decades but are insufficient in the modern environment in many ways. The research that has been done to understand why passwords are not an adequate authentication approach provides an example of how all four of the aims articulated in this report come into play. In terms of a scientific approach, one can ask what class of attacks will a given recommended password practice protect against (Aim 1)? Consider the following: The context of the password problem is usually desktops or laptops with a keyboard. A password policy for mobile phones illustrates how difficult it is to get to the right security policy. Password policies usually come with a trusted third party to help recover from losing access (by forgetting a password or having one expire). But if nobody is prepared to be a trusted third party for a phone, what should the phone do, for instance, about repeated failed log-in attempts?

Organizationally, the frequent changing of complex unique passwords has typically been touted and, in many enterprises, required as an instance of a "good security" practice. However, research on passwords belies this (Aim 4).[a] There have been empirical social science results and technical results about the effectiveness of traditional password practices. A 2010 study[b] examined password practices in a workplace and found both inflexible policies and negative impacts on productivity. Another 2010 study[c] called into question the merit of enforced password expiration. Results such as these have not always been readily translated to practice (Aim 3); however, the National Institute of Standards and Technology has developed draft rules[d] to revamp password guidelines, which, among other things, urge no expiration without reason.[e]

BOX 1.1 Continued

Is there research that can help us understand how to transition to practice such results better so as to decrease the amount of poor security practice in enterprises? Research is needed to understand broadly how to use passwords or other authentication tools in an effective way in deployed systems (Aim 3).[f] We need to authenticate users, so what are the most effective authentication mechanisms today, and what better ones can be found? And which mechanisms are most effective in which contexts? The answers to these questions depend in large part on how users perceive the need for authentication, the time and effort required to enact the authentication, and the trade-offs between authentication effort and accomplishment of the primary tasks (i.e., the actual tasks for which the users are being rewarded). All of these questions make clear that even a comparatively narrow, seemingly technical challenge such as authentication will depend on insights from multiple disciplines (Aim 2).

---

[a] C.J. Bonneau, C. Herley, P.C. van Oorschot, and F. Stajano, Passwords and the evolution of imperfect authentication, *Communications of ACM* 58(7):78-87, 2015; S.M. Bellovin and M. Merritt, "Encrypted Key Exhange: Password-Based Protocols Secure Against Dictionary Attacks," *Proceedings of the IEEE Symposium on Research in Security and Privacy*, Oakland, May 1992, https://www.cs.columbia.edu/~smb/papers/neke.pdf; P. Inglesant and M.A. Sasse, "The True Cost of Unusable Password Policies: Password Use in the Wild," *CHI 2010*, Atlanta, Ga., April 2010, https://www.cl.cam.ac.uk/~rja14/shb10/angela2.pdf; Y. Zhang, F. Monrose, and M.K. Reiter, "The Security of Modern Password Expiration: An Algorithmic Framework and Empirical Analysis," *CCS 2010*, Chicago, Ill., October 2010, http://cs.unc.edu/~fabian/papers/PasswordExpire.pdf.

[b] P. Inglesant and M.A. Sasse, "The True Cost of Unusable Password Policies: Password Use in the Wild," *CHI 2010*, Atlanta, Ga., April 2010, https://www.cl.cam.ac.uk/~rja14/shb10/angela2.pdf.

[c] Y. Zhang, F. Monrose, and M.K. Reiter, "The Security of Modern Password Expiration: An Algorithmic Framework and Empirical Analysis," *CCS 2010*, Chicago, Ill., October 2010, http://cs.unc.edu/~fabian/papers/PasswordExpire.pdf.

[d] National Institute of Standards and Technology, *Digital Identity Guidelines: Authentication and Lifecycle Management*, Draft NIST Special Publication 800-63B, https://pages.nist.gov/800-63-3/sp800-63b.html.

[e] The Federal Trade Commission has also issued guidance regarding mandatory password changes (L. Cranor, "Time to rethink mandatory password changes," Federal Trade Commission, March 2, 2016, https://www.ftc.gov/news-events/blogs/techftc/2016/03/time-rethink-mandatory-password-changes.) In addition, some of the research results were translated into U.K. government policy in the Government Communications Headquarters' (GCHQ's) revised password guidance published in 2015 (National Cyber Security Centre, "Password Guidance: Simplifying Your Approach," updated August 8, 2016, https://www.ncsc.gov.uk/guidance/password-guidance-simplifying-your-approach). GCHQ carried out a review after researchers presented a summary of results at an RISCS community meeting in London in October 2014. RISCS community meetings focus on delivery and discussion of research results and are attended by leading practitioners from GCHQ and industry. Following the debate at the community meeting, a team of GCHQ staff carried out a review, which was reviewed extensively by internal and external experts and a small set of researchers. This provides an example of how research radically changed recommended practice.

[f] A research agenda is proposed in C. Herley and P.C. van Oorschot, "A Research Agenda Acknowledging the Persistence of Passwords," *IEEE Security and Privacy Magazine*, 2012, https://www.microsoft.com/en-us/research/wp-content/uploads/2016/02/Persistence-author-copy.pdf.

or should address all four of these aims at once, articulating where a given effort sits with respect to them is important to the coherence of the research program. Security science can be thought of, broadly, as incorporating these elements (to varying degrees as appropriate), ensuring that each piece of a particular research effort meets the standards of its contributing disciplines, and integrating those efforts in coherent and disciplined ways.

This chapter has described the report's overall philosophy. Chapters 2 through 5 elaborate it. Chapter 2 examines the potential of social, behavioral, and decision sciences to contribute to improved cybersecurity. Chapter 3 highlights the importance of incorporating engineering and life-cycle considerations into the cybersecurity research endeavor. Chapter 4 outlines a foundational cybersecurity research agenda. Chapter 5 offers insights on the organization and leadership of the research community and describes opportunities to improve research practice and approach, concluding with a discussion of how the research community could reconfigure its efforts to more inclusively address cybersecurity challenges.

2

The Role of Social, Behavioral, and Decision Sciences in Security Science

Technical approaches alone will not suffice for cybersecurity insofar as humans play roles in systems as developers, users, operators, or adversaries. Major security breakdowns have occurred because individuals misplace trust, organizations create perverse incentives, or adversaries discover and exploit design flaws. Meeting security needs effectively requires understanding that human context. How does cybersecurity affect the real-world business or organization? Does it drain human or other resources, or does it reflect a balance between keeping the business or organization secure and keeping it economically viable? What investments does it deserve and receive? How does the perceived value of possible practices compare with their demonstrated efficacy? What evidence would help to make that assessment?

Social, behavioral, and decision sciences provide the reservoir of knowledge for addressing some of these questions and for making other research more useful for those responsible for vulnerable systems. Such expertise can also be vital, especially during design, in revealing any disconnects between intention and actual use and in articulating the variety of potential users and their contexts. Relevant fields include economics (e.g., incentives, resources), sociology (e.g., social networks, norms, criminology), psychology (e.g., motivation, perception, user interfaces), decision science (e.g., risk assessment, communication), linguistics (e.g., framing and conveying information), organizational psychology (e.g., multi-team systems and information sharing), political science (e.g., deterrence and international norms), and organizational behavior (e.g., recruitment, retention, reporting procedures). The law, although not a science, often synthesizes results from the sciences, with the broad integrative perspective of the humanities (see Box 2.1).

On the whole, the traditional cybersecurity community does not typically have expertise in social science analysis tools and methods. As a result, it not only relies on intuition, even when science is available, but the community also struggles in its attempts to validate its approaches and falls below scientific standards in experimental design, confounding variables, classes of confounds that occur in different domains or environments, and so on. Collaborating with social scientists and understanding their standards for research and publication would bring new tools to bear and yield new insights. The primary psychological barrier to such collaborations is that system designers and operators have unwarranted confidence in their intuitive theories regarding others' behavior (or neglect to fully consider the implications). Indeed, the human–computer interaction research community has a motto, "You are not the user," to remind researchers and practitioners not to assume that other people share their perceptions and motivations.

The primary institutional barrier to utilizing social, behavioral, and decision science expertise is that these disciplines are largely absent from the cybersecurity research community. Indeed, the community often lacks even the absorptive capacity to identify these needs, recruit the exper-

---

BOX 2.1
The Law, Policy, and Cybersecurity Research

As technology has evolved, law and policy have had to adjust to keep up with cybersecurity challenges ranging from privacy to copyright. The relevant law and policy encompass topics from basic constitutional principles related to search and freedom of speech, to regulatory efforts and statutes governing what victims of attacks can do in response, to what liability intruders and victims have in the case of an intrusion or breach. Laws and policies related to the roles and capabilities of government range from defense of government networks to intelligence and surveillance to public–private information sharing—constrain and define activity.[a] An example of a research topic in this space is the formalization of policies and regulations into models that support automated reasoning. This has been applied to security access policies and privacy-related policies. The formal models allow for an interesting interplay of human reasoning and automated reasoning.

---

[a] The Congressional Research Service notes that more than 50 statutes address various aspects of cybersecurity and that under current law, "all federal agencies have cybersecurity responsibilities relating to their own systems, and many have sector-specific responsibilities for critical infrastructure." See E.A Fischer, "Cybersecurity Issues and Challenges: In Brief," Congressional Research Service, 2016, https://www.fas.org/sgp/crs/misc/R43831.pdf.

tise needed to address them, and critically evaluate claims about system security that can be compromised by human failures in design, deployment, training, or management. Without that expertise, the cybersecurity community must improvise its own theories and research methods that are central to those sciences: experimental design, identifying confounds, meta-analysis, sensitivity analysis, and so on. Conversely, because those sciences have not been drawn into addressing the unique challenges of cybersecurity, they have limited experience in applying (and explaining) their research to those domains and in identifying the unique foundational research questions that they pose.

To create more effective collaborations, it is essential to find ways to foster interactions that address the needs of both of these disciplines and the cybersecurity community of researchers and practitioners. Part of what cross-disciplinary researchers can do is verify that use of a result in one context still holds true in another context; a result described in one environment may not be found in a different environment—and the environmental differences and their importance may not be obvious. Chapter 5 offers some programmatic suggestions for how such interactions can be encouraged. The cybersecurity community has long acknowledged and understood the gravity of issues such as insider threat and unrecognized design flaws (e.g., those inherited from legacy systems). Involving the social, behavioral, and decision sciences directly should be more effective than attempting to create cybersecurity versions of those disciplines from scratch.[1]

Approaches to security and technology need to be seen in the larger context of all that a user or organization must accomplish in the sociotechnical domain in which it operates. For instance, how can users and organizations be enabled to perform in ways that maintain security, especially when security-related tasks and activities often compete with other tasks for time and effort? Social science can illuminate what effectiveness means in terms of enabling users to get to their needed activities and accomplishments without significant time and effort spent on compliance. More importantly, rather than focus only on security mechanisms, researchers can begin or extend this kind of research by getting to the heart of why users and organizations are expected to perform security-related tasks. For example, users need to be authenticated, so what are the most effective authentication mechanisms? And which mechanisms are

---

[1] For more examples, see the August 2015 issue of *IEEE Security and Privacy*, which explored the topic of learning from other disciplines and the importance of a multidisciplinary perspective and described three case studies in which application of another discipline's techniques led to important security and privacy insights (*IEEE Security and Privacy*, 13(4), July-August 2015). See also F. Stajano and P. Wilson, Understanding scam victims: Seven principles for systems security, *Communications of the ACM* 54(3), 2011.

most effective in which contexts? The answers to these questions depend in large part on how users and organizations perceive the need for authentication, the time and effort required to enact the authentication, and the trade-offs between authentication effort and accomplishment of the primary tasks (i.e., the actual tasks for which the users are being rewarded).

Human behavior affects all stages of the life cycle of a cybersecurity system: design, implementation, evaluation, operation, maintenance, monitoring, revision, replacement, and training.[2] Each stage offers opportunities to increase or reduce vulnerability: how design teams are constituted and managed, how procedures and interfaces are tested for usability,[3] what incentives and resources are provided for security, how operators are trained and their performance evaluated, and how the business case is made and understood. Stakeholder conflicts are a well-known problem in software engineering, and there are methods for detecting and managing them that could be adapted and evaluated for conflicts involving utility, security, and usability.[4]

In the modern threat environment, cybersecurity researchers and practitioners also need to be ready for social science-based approaches being adopted by hostile adversaries and ready to respond. Box 2.2 describes how the emerging Internet of Things is an example of the multifaceted and multidisciplinary nature of the cybersecurity challenge.

One example of a project that integrated social and organizational analysis with technical research analyzed the "spam value chain."[5]

---

[2] Caputo et al. specifically studied software development and barriers to attending to security and usability needs (D.D. Caputo, S.L. Pfleeger, M.A. Sasse, P. Ammann, J. Offutt, and L. Deng, Barriers to usable security? Three organizational case studies, *IEEE Security and Privacy* 14(5): 22-32, 2016).

[3] Ivan Flechais developed the AEGIS method and UML extension to do this (I. Flechais, C. Mascolo, and M.S. Sasse, Integrating security and usability into the requirements and design process, *International Journal of Electronic Security and Digital Forensics* 1(1):12-26, 2007, doi:10.1504/IJESDF.2007.013589).

[4] In one of his last lectures at the Royal Society in 2002, Roger Needham raised the fact that security goals of the owner who pays for the system are the ones that are implemented, even if they run counter to the interests of the other stakeholders (R. Needham, Computer security? *Philosophical Transactions of the Royal Society, Series A* 361:1549-1555, 2003).

[5] K. Levchenko, A. Pitsillidis, N. Chachra, B. Enright, M. Félegyházi, C. Grier, T. Halvorson, C. Kanich, C. Kreibich, H. Liu, D. McCoy, N. Weaver, V. Paxson, G.M. Voelker, and S. Savage, "Click Trajectories: End-to-End Analysis of the Spam Value Chain," in *Proceedings of IEEE Symposium on Security and Privacy*, https://cseweb.ucsd.edu/~savage/papers/Oakland11.pdf, 2011. Stefan Savage, one of the researchers, reported on outcomes at a 2015 workshop, summarized in National Academies of Sciences, Engineering, and Medicine, *Continuing Innovation in Information Technology: Workshop Report*, The National Academies Press, Washington, D.C., 2016, p. 58:

Once alerted to the penalties of working with spammers, the banks quickly dropped these accounts, leaving spammers with no way to monetize their sales.

BOX 2.2
The Internet of Things

The Internet of Things (IoT) has emerged as a stark example of the multifaceted nature of the cybersecurity challenge. The IoT runs the gamut from voice-controlled lightbulbs in homes, to connected vehicles, to manufacturing. The security challenges in the IoT require interdisciplinary attention. For example, there are privacy concerns related to data collection and surveillance. Hardware and power constraints mean that approaches to improving security that assume plentiful computing capacity or readily available network connectivity and power will not apply. At the same time, IoT dramatically expands the range of domains in which cybersecurity is needed and the range of organizations and institutions that will deploy IoT systems. From health care, to building security, to home appliances, user expectations and systems requirements will vary widely as will the economics of IoT, which often involves inexpensive devices that are updated rarely, if at all.

Companies that sell some types of software, such as desktop office programs, expect a continuing engagement with their customers. So they build systems in a way that upgrade is possible, make investments to repair vulnerabilities, and distribute those repairs (for a fee or not). The business model of some of today's IoT companies is not based on ongoing support of a product once it has been sold. Moreover, for most applications, an IoT company (as opposed to a desktop operating system company) may have a more difficult time attracting security experts because there would not be a career-growth plan for that skill set within the company.

The IoT also poses challenges for regulatory and governmental institutions because they can be used as vectors to attack other systems, as was seen in recent botnet attacks that took advantage of unsecured routers, cameras, and other devices.[a] In those circumstances, neither the user nor the manufacturer has a stake in the security problem.

---

[a] Krebs on Security, "Source Code for IoT Botnet 'Mirai' Released," October 1, 2016, https://krebsonsecurity.com/2016/10/source-code-for-iot-botnet-mirai-released/

Researchers discovered that a significant majority of transactions for spam-advertised products were handled by a very small number of companies. As a result, they identified a nontechnical chokepoint in the system where a combination of a policy and financial mechanisms (refusing to authorize credit card payments for those companies) significantly reduced the amount of spam on the Internet. Spam up to that point had been seen primarily as a technical identification and filtering problem.

While switching e-mails or domains is easy, switching banks is far more difficult for spammers, and this strategy has proved effective in shutting down certain types of spammers. As a result, there has been a substantial drop in sales of pirated software as a whole.

The rest of this chapter discusses how social, behavioral, and decision sciences can contribute to research in cybersecurity and to security science; provides a preliminary list of areas that provide opportunities for collaboration; and examines in more detail two specific topics of particular importance to cybersecurity: (1) incentives and resources and (2) risk analysis. The chapter concludes with a discussion of opportunities to improve prospects for interdisciplinary work in cybersecurity.

CONTRIBUTIONS FROM SOCIAL, BEHAVIORAL, AND DECISION SCIENCES

Collaborating with social, behavioral, and decision scientists would put their substantive theories and methodological procedures at the service of the cybersecurity community. Achieving that integration will, however, require a sustained commitment. Without it, though, these scientists will not develop the working relationships needed to achieve and deserve the trust of cybersecurity researchers and practitioners. Nor will they have the incentive to broaden their traditional pursuits in order to master cybersecurity topics and translate them into terms recognizable by their colleagues. Unless researchers trained in these disciplines become part of the cybersecurity research community, its members will be forced to continue to do the best they can to find and interpret the relevant literature.[6]

Results and approaches from other disciplines can help improve cybersecurity research and ultimately cybersecurity outcomes. For instance, research in other domains has documented that people do not have a perfect understanding of threats and can be oblivious to some kinds of threats, and has documented how to afford them the mental models and incentives needed for better risk perceptions. Social scientists study the human determinants of trust. They find, for example, that people tend to anthropomorphize technical systems and look for cues similar to what they would get in a human interaction. Research into e-mail and "flaming" in the 1980s, when e-mail became popular, revealed this.[7] People do not appreciate how much information was eliminated when voice and in-person interactions were restricted to plain text. There is research available for many of those sorts of human topics and behaviors. In this example, what are the aspects of trust in human–system interactions that

---

[6] The Computing Research Association recognized the value and importance of these disciplines to computing broadly in a 2015 letter to the House Science Committee (available at http://cra.org/govaffairs/blog/2015/04/cra-statement-opposing-america-competes-reauthorization-act/).

[7] S. Kiesler, J. Siegel, and T.W. McGuire, Social psychological aspects of computer-mediated communication, *American Psychologist* 39:1123-1134, 1984.

would never have occurred to the people who would study trust in the full-bandwidth, interpersonal situation? Those researchers studying interpersonal communication on e-mail asked questions that had not occurred to social psychologists before because there was this new environment that manipulated or constrained people's behavior in a way that had not occurred to that field before. Researchers might not have been able to make progress on the question of interpersonal trust without technology. And new technology-mediated forms of communication continue to pose new challenges to trust between humans. This illustrates a way in which cybersecurity challenges can offer new opportunities for social scientists to explore their own theories.[8]

With regard to large-scale systems such as today's cloud-based services, an example of the cross-cutting nature of the cybersecurity problem relates to a broader sense of *trust*. How should trust and expectations regarding trust, as they exist in an enterprise or between institutions, be realigned in a digital context? Many information systems treat trust as transitive (if entity A trusts B, and B trusts C, then A also trusts C), but, of course, trust does not work the same way or mean the same thing in interpersonal, social, or organizational contexts. Moreover, users of such systems may have little idea what string of relationships underlies any direct relationship.

The lack of bandwidth mentioned above does not provide a complete explanation, however. Even in non-computer-mediated interactions, people look for efficiencies and use trust cues as shortcuts to carrying out a full risk and benefit assessment. For instance, consumers do not read all reviews of a store they might visit. Instead, they quickly scan whether it is well stocked, if staff are appropriately helpful and trained (all signs of investment), and, last, whether the other customers are similar to themselves. Once they have had a successful experience, they expect that store to deliver in the future. This approach works reasonably reliably in the physical world, but may not be as reliable online where it is inexpensive for adversaries to mimic trust cues and impersonate others. People bring their trust models from the physical world and do not always realize that they do not apply in the online environment. The recently revealed hacks of major political figures show vulnerability and consequences for even (or perhaps especially) prominent individuals.

---

[8] See, for instance, J. Steinke, B. Bolunmez, L. Fletcher, V. Wang, A.J. Tomassetti, K.M. Repchik, S.J. Zaccaro, R.S. Dalal, and L.E. Tetrick, Improving cybersecurity incident response team effectiveness using teams-based research, *IEEE Security and Privacy* 13:20-29, 2015. This work applies theories about multi-team systems to cybersecurity incident response teams. Not only has that work tested existing theories; it has also led to new processes for documenting multi-team systems, whether or not they involve cybersecurity.

BUILDING COLLABORATIVE COMMUNITIES

Designing competent socio-technical systems will necessarily encompass multiple disciplines (see Box 2.3 for a list of such topics). Although there are promising subcommunities within computer science and related disciplines,[9] there are significant barriers to such collaboration. Crossing disciplinary boundaries requires deep, sustained participation from researchers in the relevant disciplines, not just expecting experts in one area to cover topics outside their home discipline or to work in parallel, hoping that the pieces mesh.

If the cybersecurity community is to engage social scientists, there must be compelling reasons why research in cybersecurity would enhance their careers. These incentives may include providing a pathway for publication in social science venues that can lead to tenure and promotion, as well as framing projects so that graduate students can be involved and use the results for doctoral dissertations. Such collaborations are not natural acts for researchers in most communities. As a result, it may be useful to engage researchers who are already well versed in several disciplines to act as "translators" on cross-disciplinary projects. Thus, cybersecurity researchers should not be expected to become experts in social science research, but they need to understand the kinds of controls and quality assurance mechanisms that it requires.

Moreover, it is not likely to be fruitful to expect cybersecurity researchers to learn about the findings of other disciplines on their own. Indeed, it can be dangerous if they read a single paper (or worse, a secondary account) without knowing the context for the reported finding—how strong it is, how consistent with other research. More productive would be to find ways to foster interactions with other disciplines so that cybersecurity researchers and practitioners can describe the elements of the problems needing solutions, and researchers from other disciplines can identify those aspects of their disciplines that might be useful in providing insights or solutions. It is the job of a researcher in a given discipline to know the literature and implications of that discipline. This avoids the risk of cybersecurity researchers reading small bits of the literature of that discipline, potentially out of context, and applying results inappropriately. Part of what the cross-disciplinary teams do is verify that a result observed in one context still holds true in another, considering differences that may not be obvious to those without professional training. The institutional challenge is to support social, behavioral, and decision science experts as equal partners when working on cybersecurity research

---

[9] See, for example, the Symposium on Usable Privacy and Security (https://cups.cs.cmu.edu/soups/), the Workshop on the Economics of Information Security (http://econinfosec.org/), and the Privacy Enhancing Technologies Symposium (https://petsymposium.org/).

BOX 2.3
Some Social, Behavioral, and Decision Science
Topics Relevant to Security Science

- Macroeconomics and its implications for the national economy and government investments.
- Microeconomics and individual incentives—users, developers, vendors, and others.
- Human factors—usability design and testing; complementing vs. replacing operators.
- Behavioral psychology and its implications for decision making, assessment of trust, vulnerabilities, user behavior (and user behavior in response to system- or management-imposed rules),[a] and so on.
- Legal and regulatory theory—understanding regulation as both technology supporting and suppressing and interactions with political realities.
- Impacts of corporate governance, boards, and policies on cybersecurity expectations, practices, and policies.
- Political science and the roles of citizens as operators, users, developers, and political actors.
- Political science and international relations and issues of conflict, deterrence, war, and norms.
- Organizational theory and how competent organizations develop policies, training, rewards, and culture.
- International relations theory and implications for conflict and non-technical measures (norms, treaties, signaling) for addressing it.

---

[a] Recent access, actions, and disclosures by, for example, Edward Snowden, Chelsea Manning, and others highlight the systemic risk in single-person permission and access to vast collections of secure files in dispersed locations. Assessment and better understanding and measurement of the systemic or behavioral risk of high-level access by single or cooperative multiple antagonists is an important aspect of the security challenge.

---

efforts.[10] The point of a meaningful and sustained cross-disciplinary effort is collaboration (not consultation).

INCENTIVES, RESOURCES, AND RISK IN CYBERSECURITY

This section examines in more detail two specific topics of particular importance to cybersecurity practices in real-world environments: (1) incentives and resources and (2) risk analysis.

---

[10] The research community in the United Kingdom has endeavored to develop such a community in the Research Institute in Science of Cyber Security: Researchers present results to practitioners, and practitioners present challenges and questions. If the questions cannot be addressed with existing results, a discussion ensues that in many cases leads to new research studies or projects to investigate those questions.

Understanding Incentives and Resources

Incentives for attackers and, separately, for the industry and market-place as a whole are constantly in flux. Resources are limited, and investments need to be made carefully. One challenge is to understand when cybersecurity measures are worth investing in and when investments in other capabilities would improve security for an organization. Insights from the social sciences can help in making this determination. For instance, an analysis of airport security efforts suggests that sometimes investing in improving non-security aspects of the systems can improve security more than security measures.[11] Even considering the narrower challenge of specifically cyber-related attacks and defenses, examining resource availability for each can be instructive. That examination should consider the incentives shaping the cybersecurity actions of all actors, from the most casual "script kiddies" to the most competent agencies of first-rate powers. Every attack has desired outcomes, and the more resources (money, time, opportunity costs) required to acheive those outcomes, the fewer of those outcomes there will be. Understanding resource constraints on the part of attackers can help with planning and decision making, and can help focus research activity.

A commonly repeated claim is that defenders have to defend every-thing all the time, but the attackers only have to be successful once, mean-ing that defenders must expend significantly more resources than attackers, especially if attackers are trading information and tools. However, there is a symmetric proposition that sometimes applies: Defenders only have to catch an attack once and make changes that thwart it worldwide, after which the attacker's work to exploit that vulnerability becomes much more difficult, not just in terms of the expense of the immediate engagement, but possibly also in terms of consumption of "zero days."[12]

But for this to be true, the defenders have to understand the spe-cific techniques used in the attack (so-called indicators of compromise), develop and implement protective measures, and share that information with people and organizations capable of using it. And those individuals and organizations have to be incentivized to apply the appropriate reme-diations. Construction of defenses can include mechanisms whereby defenders not only repel an attack, but also engage with sensors, deflec-tion, and other processes that enable them to gain useful information related to the methods, motives, and identities of attackers through the

---

[11] H. Molotch, *Against Security: How We Go Wrong at Airports, Subways, and Other Sites of Ambiguous Danger*, Princeton University Press, Princeton, N.J., 2012.

[12] A "zero day" is a vulnerability that has not been publicly disclosed or reported before being exploited. The term refers to the amount of time (zero days) available to create fixes or work-arounds before the exploit becomes active.

process of an engagement. Unfortunately, too many organizations do not (or cannot) benefit from such knowledge when it is developed and are thus incapable of contributing to the common defense.

Another example of how incentives affect cybersecurity and might benefit from such research is how to secure an infrastructure that depends on components developed by the open-source community. How can open-source developers be incentivized to use better tools and practices in the development of software, particularly safety and security-critical software? More specifically, how can they be incentivized to audit or rewrite older code as new classes of vulnerabilities come to light? One potential advantage of open source is the tremendous sharing of tools and practices within the community. As a result, investments from industry and government stakeholders are likely to yield broad benefit—and also influence vendor organizations, commercial tool developers, and so on. What should be the obligations of those who use open-source software in their systems?

One effort under way to address open-source software security is the Linux Foundation's Core Infrastructure Initiative, which was set up in the aftermath of the discovery of the Heartbleed vulnerability in OpenSSL. The processes in place allowed a single developer to make updates over a holiday with just a cursory review by a "committer" before being added to the codebase. There were only a handful of developers responsible for software that underpins much online commerce activity. In addition, major corporations were running systems that depended on that component, and the extent of that dependence was either not realized or was not seen as a significant risk by risk analysts or auditors in those corporations. That vulnerability revealed a number of ways in which a combination of technical, social, and organizational decisions and practices led to a significant problem.

The initiative is set up to bring organizations that depend on open-source software together with open-source development communities with the aim of improving practice. It provides funding for individual developers to work on improving the security of their projects and is also grappling with the problem of how to improve practices more broadly. This initiative and its results are an opportunity to understand better what processes, technologies, and structures make efforts to maintain and improve open-source projects effective.

Risk Analysis

A formal risk analysis provides a way to organize information about different kinds of weaknesses a system may have—from implementation errors to inadequate backup and recovery mechanisms—and the kinds of threats that may exploit those weaknesses. It helps indicate whether sufficient resources, or too many resources, are being applied to mitigating vulnerabilities, preparing for recovery, and so on. Assessments of vulnerabilities and the likely costs of an effective response are both made in the context of threat assumptions, which also need to be characterized as part of the analysis, as do consequences.

There are essentially two ways to conduct a risk analysis.[13] One is to evaluate relative risk of competing procedures and operational decisions in a given system and to understand implications of changes in the system (e.g., design, operation, maintenance) and its operating environment (e.g., tasks, adversaries, threats). This evaluation can clarify how the system works, how to manage it, and how to evaluate the quality of competing approaches. The toolkit for such analyses includes systematic analyses of existing performance data, translation of existing research into model terms, and disciplined expert elicitation.[14] A much more ambitious way of using risk analysis is to try to assess the absolute level of risk in a system. Often, the latter is unproductive or even counterproductive, as it leads to large, complicated, unreviewable projects with an incentive to leave out things that are not easily quantified. Indeed, in 2013, Langner and Pederson argued that without effective ways to calculate risk, managers will always underestimate it and choose to underinvest in security.[15] Instead, they will invest in other areas that they understand better and that will lead to clear payoffs (e.g., profits, better service, or improved efficiency, depending on the kind of organization).

Conducted appropriately, risk analysis provides an orderly way of putting diverse kinds of information on a common platform. Risk analysis can inform system design by creating a transparent platform for sharing assumptions about performance of the system's elements and their interdependencies. It forces thinking about the metrics that are relevant to a decision maker. Often things that are readily countable are not the things that are most important. And, as will be discussed in Chapter 4, metrics regarding cybersecurity have been notoriously difficult to develop. Effective risk analysis can provide tools for structuring and understanding what information can be collected. Risk analysis requires inputs from experts in all the factors affecting system performance, integrated with the

---

[13] See B. Fischhoff, The realities of risk-cost-benefit analysis, *Science* 350(6260):527, 2015; and B. Fischhoff and J. Kadvany, *Risk: A Very Short Introduction*, Oxford University Press, Oxford, U.K., 2011.

[14] M.G. Morgan, Use (and abuse) of expert elicitation in support of decision making for public policy, *Proceedings of the National Academy of Sciences* 111(20):7176–7184, 2014.

[15] R. Langner and P. Pederson, "Bound to Fail: Why Cyber Security Risk Cannot Be 'Managed' Away," Brookings Institution, 2013, https://www.brookings.edu/research/bound-to-fail-why-cyber-security-risk-cannot-be-managed-away/.

analytical tools of decision science. The result is a transparent platform for summarizing, evaluating, and communicating the state of system knowledge. This type of risk analysis is not done widely in cybersecurity, and research here has high potential payoff in taking fullest advantage of knowledge in security science.

MAKING PROGRESS

The committee identified barriers to collaboration both within and among the disciplines and recommends strategic institutional initiatives to overcome them. It also identifies some promising initiatives to integrate social and behavioral sciences into cybersecurity. One is the National Science Foundation's (NSF's) Secure and Trustworthy Cyberspace portfolio, which is a cross-cutting effort that explicitly includes social and behavioral science. Another recent NSF effort laid out a vision for experimental cybersecurity research that urges a culture of experimentation, an emphasis on multidisciplinarity, grounding basic work in real-world systems, and recognizing the range of human actors who shape system performance.[16]

More can be done to improve prospects for and outcomes of interdisciplinary research. There are many barriers to effective and ongoing integration of disparate research cultures. In particular, although individual researchers and research projects can look for ways to work across disciplines, sustained long-term efforts that build on results over time and continue to integrate new results from other disciplines will require support and commitment from both the research community and research funders. Knowledge regarding user and organizational incentives for or obstacles to implementing changes in practice and policies is needed for such changes to be put into place. An assertive approach to multidisciplinary integration could lead to a culture of foundational research that involves a conscious and sustained interplay between technical advances and incorporating results from the social and behavioral sciences about how to change systems, developer practices, user expectations, and institutional policies.

---

[16] D. Balenson, L. Tinnel, and T. Benzel, *Cybersecurity Experimentation of the Future (CEF): Catalyzing a New Generation of Experimental Cybersecurity Research*, 2015, http://www.cyberexperimentation.org/files/5514/3834/3934/CEF_Final_Report_20150731.pdf.

3

Engineering, Operational, and Life-Cycle Challenges in Security Science

Improving cybersecurity requires that security considerations be integrated into the practice of hardware and software development, evolution, deployment, and evaluation—indeed, to reflect an understanding of the life cycle of a system. Research in many technical areas may embed assumptions (e.g., about agility and expected operations and maintenance) or may be focused explicitly on how to improve post-deployment activities related to systems. That is, research that focuses on how maintenance and system administration affect overall system performance would be part of a holistic approach to cybersecurity. Improved cybersecurity requires good technology control, resilience, and reliability, highlighting the importance of research in software quality assurance as well as more traditional notions of software security research.

LESSONS FROM DEVELOPMENT ORGANIZATIONS

In addition to what the traditional industrial research and academic communities contribute, software development organizations developing commodity systems have made substantial efforts to improve their own practices and the systems they build. These organizations have, over time, created a set of development practices aimed at reducing the prevalence of exploitable vulnerabilities in released software.[1] A critical

---

[1] For example, see, Microsoft, "What is the Security Development Lifecycle?," 2016, https://www.microsoft.com/en-us/sdl/default.aspx, accessed September 2016. See also M. Howard and S. Lipner, *The Security Development Lifecycle: A Process for Developing Demon-*

component of these approaches is the use of feedback loops from discovered vulnerabilities or attacks that are traced to root causes. Applied systematically, these feedback loops can lead to new tools or techniques and are fundamental to improving cybersecurity. These efforts can be part of security science, integrating what is known about state-of-the-art software engineering practices; social, behavioral, and organizational theory; current understandings of the threat landscape; and models of attacks and defenses. Practical lessons from companies working at the cutting edge of secure system development can inform research approaches that incorporate scientific models. There are also opportunities to use well-established open-source projects as raw material for analysis (e.g., use of software life-cycle data). In academia, some of this sort of work has been done using open-source software as a source of information as well as working with large software companies.[2] The open-source stacks offer for study an abundance of components, libraries, frameworks, and tools. There is also a strong tradition of data analysis of open-source repository data and other data. And, most obviously, in most open-source projects, there is ready access to code, design documents, test cases, analysis models, process data, historical data, and so on.

Recently, the National Institute of Standards and Technology issued a report exploring how to reduce technical vulnerabilities in software.[3] It offers an analysis of a number of technical approaches that can be applied in the software development process, their potential impacts, and suggestions for encouraging the development and use of a number of measurements and metrics to help assess software. Research on how security outcomes relate to development practices and on the use of particular tools and software languages is foundational. Cybersecurity outcomes ultimately rely on the properties of the systems developed and deployed in the real world. If it is known, for instance, that a certain class of programming languages and their compilers can prevent a wide class of

---

strably More Secure Software, Microsoft Press, Redmond, Wash., 2006. Microsoft has been especially open regarding its tooling and quality efforts—features include (1) diversity of models and tools, (2) clear pathways and incentives for development teams to adopt improved practices without coercion of a mandate, and (3) a creative approach to assessment of benefits and costs.

[2] For example, see Laurie Williams' research group's efforts to study software security using empirical analysis (A. Konovalov, "Project Zero," blog, May 10, 2007, https://googleprojectzero.blogspot.com/ undertakes security analysis and publishes regularly on weaknesses in vendor projects).

[3] P.E. Black, L. Badger, B. Guttman, and E. Fong, Dramatically Reducing Software Vulnerabilities: Report to the White House Office of Science and Technology Policy, National Institute of Standards and Technology, 2016, http://csrc.nist.gov/publications/drafts/nistir-8151/nistir8151_draft.pdf.

common errors[4] that lead to security vulnerabilities, how can their wide
adoption be incentivized? Managed languages and compilers have been
explored and developed through research. Understanding which class of
errors they prevent is related to the scientific foundations discussed in
Chapter 1. Understanding how to incentivize their adoption would draw
on social science knowledge and research. An additional challenge is
that developers of systems frequently reuse software components developed by others, including components affecting security. Vulnerabilities
in these components can result in common vulnerabilities across many
systems.[5] Even when the developers of the components fix vulnerabilities,
the revisions may not result in updates to all the systems that depend on
them. It would be worth understanding how often this occurs, especially
in the Internet of Things (IoT) and other embedded devices. One might
reverse-engineer the software in many different devices to estimate the
distribution of shared components and how current they are.

Another operational challenge is virtualization. As the use of virtualization increases, it is important that security is addressed as an integral
part of the technology and the architecture that is being virtualized. This
spans the use of various hypervisors in infrastructures to the container
approaches to application security. As security is increasingly integrated
into virtualized environments, a recurring research challenge is how to
assess and measure the effectiveness, completeness, and effective integration of the security measures.

LESSONS FROM REAL-WORLD DEPLOYMENTS

System administrators and other practitioners are often on the front
lines of securing systems. It is important to develop mechanisms whereby

---

[4] For instance, in the Defense Advanced Research Projects Agency's clean-slate total-
system architecture research and development effort on a new capability-based hardware,
new operating systems and low-level compartmentalization kernels, and extensions of
common programming languages that reflect the capability mechanism, it is the LLVM
compiler extensions that address the hardware and inherently prevent buffer overflows
and numerous other common security flaws. See D. Chisnall, C. Rothwell, B. Davis, R.N.M.
Watson, J. Woodruff, S.W. Moore, P.G. Neumann, and M. Roe, "Beyond the PDP-11: Archi-
tectural Support for a Memory-Safe C Abstract Machine," 20th International Conference on
Architectural Support for Programming Languages and Operating Systems, ASPLOS 2015,
Istanbul, Turkey, March 14-18, 2015; and R.N.M. Watson, J. Woodruff, P.G. Neumann, S.W.
Moore, J. Anderson, D. Chisnall, N. Dave, B. Davis, B. Laurie, S.J. Murdoch, R. Norton, M.
Roe, S. Son, and M. Vadera, "CHERI: A Hybrid Capability-System Architecture for Scalable
Software Compartmentalization," IEEE Symposium on Security and Privacy, San Jose, Calif.,
May 18-20, 2015.
[5] One example is the continued use of Windows XP in some embedded applications.
OpenSSL is another.

researchers can learn about the real problems being experienced in the field by practitioners. Example areas of overlap include work on resilient architectures, composition of components and properties, logging systems, variability, and configuration. Researchers in these areas benefit hugely from industry contacts and trust relationships with practitioner colleagues. In cybersecurity, however, knowledge transfer can be difficult, since so much is sensitive, including information about vulnerabilities, threats, events, data affected, organizational impacts, roles of human actors, and so on. In addition, understanding industry norms and expectations, and how they are evolving, is important. For instance, requirements for improved measurement and evaluation regimes will likely have an impact on practices and will need to be accounted for in research.

Related to the topic of observation, vulnerability research is an area that examines existing, deployed computer systems and networks with the aim of discovering new vulnerabilities. (See Box 3.1 for background on how this community developed.) The vulnerability "hacker" research ecosystem is often considered distinct from academic research, but it is clearly not. There are opportunities for academic researchers to learn from vulnerability research and to collaborate with vulnerability researchers. There are also open research questions—technical questions regarding the science of vulnerability finding (e.g., code-focused research based on binaries, directed fuzzing,[6] and low-level analysis as well as such research based on source-level considerations, design of runtime application programming interfaces [APIs], and so on) as well as social science questions regarding motivating and rewarding vulnerability researchers to maximize the likelihood that newly found vulnerabilities or classes of vulnerabilities will be mitigated or eliminated from systems rather than being exploited. For instance, how effective are so-called bug bounties in terms of improving the security of systems? How do results from bug bounty efforts compare to other efforts? In terms of communications and reporting, vulnerability research results could be strengthened by including an estimate of the practical effect of what has been discovered. More generally, how can threat information play into this part of the process? There is a set of questions related to understanding attackers and deriving attack trees.[7] Deriving attack trees can be helpful in considering whether an artifact satisfies its specification and how complete the specification itself is. For instance, are there implicit assumptions that lead to

---

[6] Fuzzing or fuzz testing is a way of testing software by providing large amounts of random or unexpected data to a system to try to make it crash. Directed fuzzing is a variation by which key parts of well-formed input are determined, and those are modified (fuzzed)—for instance, to ensure that fuzzed input can get past basic checksums.

[7] An attack tree is a diagram used to describe how a target might be attacked. It can be used to show the many different paths that could lead to a successful attack.

BOX 3.1
Vulnerability Research Community

Although the computing research community has a long history of studying systems for flaws and vulnerabilities, the growth of the Internet and Internet-connected computer systems has enlisted an expanding community of individuals who search for flaws, especially in newly available systems, and report oversights to their developers. That reporting includes private reports, publication in Internet newsgroups, and sale to vulnerable individuals or organizations. While some of these vulnerability researchers confined themselves to repeated attempts to find simple errors, others found new classes of vulnerabilities that, once discovered, proved to represent common and serious threats to Internet-connected systems. For example, Elias Levy (Aleph One) published "Smashing the Stack for Fun and Profit" in the online hacker magazine *Phrack* in 1996 and gave birth to the wide understanding and exploitation of buffer overruns in programs written in the programming languages C and C++.

The number of vulnerability researchers grew with the importance of protecting Internet-connected systems and ongoing discoveries of vulnerabilities that had real-world impact. In the late 1990s and early 2000s, start-up companies built security product and consulting service businesses based on their staffs' reputations as expert vulnerability finders and their claims that their products could protect users from exploitation of the vulnerabilities they had discovered or their services could help to root out vulnerabilities in products or systems.

Collaboration and sharing of techniques and results has always been encouraged within the community. Early collaborations began with private mailing lists and informal in-person gatherings. Over time, the gatherings grew into a worldwide array of "hacker conferences" such as Black Hat and DefCon (probably the largest with more than 10,000 attendees), Hack in the Box, CanSecWest, 44Con, and numerous others. The results reported at these conferences range from known vulnerabilities in new kinds of systems (e.g., hacking connected automobiles), to new classes of vulnerabilities, to new techniques for finding or mitigating vulnerabilities. Some hacker conferences present results by academic researchers, and a few academic security conferences (such as the IEEE Symposium on Security and Privacy) present results that could as well be reported at hacker conferences—so the distinction between academic and hacker/vulnerability research is blurring. In addition, there has been attention to tools that can automate both the development of exploits and the launching of attacks.

Today, many organizations that are interested in improving the security of their products mobilize the vulnerability research community with "bug bounties." These bounties pay financial rewards to individuals or organizations that discover new vulnerabilities and report them so they can be corrected. Microsoft has sought to use bug bounties to improve product security by paying bounties for discoveries of bugs in prerelease software and by providing significant financial rewards to researchers who find ways to mitigate new classes of vulnerabilities. (At least one "mitigation bounty" was paid to a graduate student researcher.) Many companies and other organizations pay bounties for discovery of vulnerabilities in shipping products (e.g., Google and Apple) or operational online services (e.g., the Department of Defense, United Airlines). An open research question is whether legitimate bug bounties expand the supply of zero-day exploits available to malicious actors who can offer higher bounties or contract the supply by discovering and fixing vulnerabilities before they can be exploited.

vulnerabilities? This sort of analysis connects vulnerability and life-cycle analyses with formal verification approaches to yield a more complete understanding of the security of a system.

CHALLENGES OF CYBERSECURITY METRICS

One cross-cutting technical challenge involves metrics.[8] Developing a metric of the "overall cybersecurity" of a system is very difficult to do, not least because what is meant by "security" can vary significantly.[9] At a minimum, such a global metric would require a comprehensive model of the system in question. But adversaries can exploit vulnerabilities in deployed systems, whose detailed characteristics may not all be captured by a model, meaning that a global cybersecurity metric defined on a model may not capture all possible attacks. Moreover, as Herley observes, the fact that there is no single observation that would allow an arbitrary system to be declared secure shows that claims of necessary conditions for security are unfalsifiable.[10] Instead, one can exclude various vulnerabilities.

One can think in terms of what sorts of failures are allowed. For example, is the goal to minimize maximum regret, minimize average regret, maximize time between successful attacks of any sort, or something else? Regardless of the attack vector, is the goal to have a system where the attack surface is relatively large but where damage of a successful attack is limited, or a system where the attack surface is relatively small but where damage is catastrophic if an attack succeeds? Put another way, given fixed resources, should one set up a highly regimented, centrally controlled homogeneous infrastructure that is well administered or a federated heterogeneous infrastructure that may not be as well administered? The latter obviously has a larger attack surface, assuming appropriate independence, but the former is more susceptible to complete compromise once penetrated. The larger observation is that security is not only non-binary—it does not lend itself to a linear ordering. This makes the concept of security metrics even more difficult.

---

[8] See S.M. Bellovin, On the brittleness of software and the infeasibility of security metrics, *IEEE Security and Privacy*, 2006.

[9] Pfleeger and Cunningham have written at length about why security is difficult to measure. See S.L. Pfleeger and R. Cunningham, Why measuring security is hard, *IEEE Security and Privacy* 8(4):46-54, 2010, http://doi.ieeecomputersociety.org/10.1109/MSP.2010.60.

[10] C. Herley, Unfalsifiability of security claims, *Proceedings of the National Academies of Sciences* 113(23):6415-6420, 2016. The ideas in this paper were followed up and expanded on in C. Herley and P. van Oorschot, "SoK: Science, Security, and the Elusive Science of Security," *Proceedings of the 2017 IEEE Symposium on Security and Privacy*, forthcoming, http://people.scs.carleton.ca/~paulv/papers/oakland2017science.pdf.

There are properties of systems and of organizations that can be measured and can serve as a useful proxy against known classes of attacks. Proxy measures can be valuable as a way to distinguish between the cybersecurity equivalent of biomarkers (e.g., elements of blood chemistry) and health states (e.g., vision problems related to diabetes). Good biomarkers can be valuable, even essential, for monitoring latent conditions and monitoring conditions that are difficult to assess directly (whereas bad ones can be distractions or misleading in dangerous ways).

Metrics to measure capabilities of organizations could be developed. Examples of such metrics include the following: Does the organization use publicly available indicators of compromise? For what fraction of its systems and network? Does the organization collect data flows on its internal network and external connections? Another aspect that might be subject to measurement is commitment to continuous improvement. Does the organization learn from its own (and others') mistakes and adapt? Over what kind of time frame?

Research is needed on metrics that make clear what could be done in terms of organizational practices. In many cases, which practices enhance security in a given context is not known. Most organizations have limited resources to devote to security. Researchers have an opportunity to investigate the degree to which each security practice is successful in a given context. One goal would be to provide practitioners with an understanding of what improvements and returns on investment an organization could expect for given security practices (and for how long and under what conditions). This kind of research needs the involvement of social scientists—and especially organizational psychologists, who can characterize the organizations, the people in them, and their practices and offer ways to assess the impacts of new practices. Another benefit would be to publicly describe the measures practiced by the most successful organizations in a way that makes them available for use as metrics by others. Further, this work would need to be kept up-to-date. Adversaries change tactics and approaches frequently, and the organizations who successfully defend themselves adapt continuously. Moving toward better ways to describe and measure security and security-related properties of a system and of organizations will involve understanding how science, models, attacks, and defenses interact; how systems are engineered, deployed, and maintained; and how organizations decide to invest in, develop, and promulgate technologies, practices, and policies regarding security.

ADDITIONAL RESEARCH TOPICS

Achieving effective outcomes stems from a combination of understanding models of systems, communicating that understanding well across the research community, applying research results, high-quality engineering, understanding deployed systems, and a host of social, organizational, and behavioral considerations. In addition to development practices and engineering that prioritize security in the features and functionality of a system, designing systems for a complete life cycle that includes secure procurement, use, maintenance, operations, system administration, and aftermarket activities (such as notifications, updates, and repairs) is an important consideration. Legacy systems exist and will continue to be used—there is a research opportunity regarding how better to secure them and technical challenges that range from system-level reverse engineering to sandboxing to service-oriented architectures.

In addition to the ideas discussed above, potential topics of research and exploration include the following:

- Improving the inspectability of trusted subsystems—for example, by incorporating security checks (e.g., checksums of common software components across an enterprise) into regular operations and administration to watch for unexpected changes.
- Establishing and maintaining a root of trust and configuration integrity.
- Exploring architectural considerations such as coupling and minimization of the trusted computing bases, API and framework design issues, resiliency, pervasive monitoring and logging, and so on.
- Using a "DevOps" approach where developers and operators are collaborating to improve the security of cloud-based services. (The increased use of cloud-based software services has some security advantages—for instance, it is much easier to update the software as needed. On the other hand, the capability to roll out updates and changes rapidly can lead to mistakes that happen at scale, and the security and privacy risks at scale may weigh against cost savings.)
- Continuing to improve the ecosystem by which (sanitized) data sets from industry can be shared with cybersecurity experts in academia such that long-term empirical studies can be conducted that will allow a wide range of cybersecurity metrics to be tracked and for formal experiments that test particular research hypotheses to be conducted.
- Increasing the resilience of up-front engineering for embedded systems, SCADA systems, and the IoT. In these cases, updates are infrequent, if they are ever done. What incentives are available to make such engineering happen? Or, if these systems are made more easily "update-able," how can their use as an attack channel

be prevented? And how can users be provided with a high level of confidence that updating will not negatively impact their systems?

- Developing scientific models that incorporate assumptions about anticipated longevity and usage expectations.
- Designing and evaluating the usability of systems (readable user messages, careful selection of the options presented, careful design and selection of the metaphors through which policies and status are communicated to humans, and so on).
- Developing effective ways for cybersecurity experts, system administrators, and others who operate the systems to share insights and learn from each other regarding, for instance, designing and testing security protocols, data logging and analysis, and so on.
- Working with the operations and engineering communities to begin to understand "ground truth" about what is actually deployed and operating in the real world. For instance, to what extent do embedded systems or the IoT share security-relevant components and code? This would require systematic surveys, analysis, and reporting, and possibly include the need to reverse-engineer code.
- Developing better linkages between research and standards and evaluation criteria for cybersecurity.
- Considering observation itself as a fundamental scientific approach and developing an ongoing, realistic understanding of what the universe of deployed systems looks and behaves like through the use of monitoring, logging, and data analysis (real-time, lagged, and forensic) to inform ongoing cybersecurity research efforts and priorities.

4

Foundational Research Topics

Numerous research agendas for cybersecurity have been developed and promulgated. For instance, a decade ago the National Research Council report *Toward a Safer and More Secure Cyberspace*[1] argued that both traditional and unorthodox approaches to research are needed in order to create new knowledge and to make that knowledge usable and transferable. That report also emphasized the importance of breadth and diversity in research agendas, because the risks will be on the rise for the foreseeable future, and a broad, diverse research agenda will increase the likelihood that a useful approach to address some future threat can be found. That approach is still relevant today, as cybersecurity challenges have only increased over time.

More recently, the federal Networking and Information Technology Research and Development Program issued its *Federal Cybersecurity Research and Development Strategic Plan.*[2] That plan rests on four assumptions related to adversaries, defenders, users, and technology; outlines a number of near-, mid-, and long-term goals; spotlights four defensive elements: deter, protect, detect, and adapt; outlines six critical areas, the first three of which are most relevant to this report: scientific foundations, enhancements in risk management, and human aspects; and offers five

---

[1] National Research Council, *Toward a Safer and More Secure Cyberspace*, The National Academies Press, Washington, D.C., 2007.

[2] National Science and Technology Council, *Federal Cybersecurity Research and Development Strategic Plan: Ensuring Prosperity and National Security*, Networking and Information Technology Research and Development Program, February 2016.

recommendations for the federal government, the first of which is to prioritize basic and long-term research.

This report is intended to complement the strategic plan—it emphasizes and elaborates on several specific components of the plan and offers a distinctive framework through which to view research efforts. This section offers a research agenda that can be mapped to components of the strategic plan. However, as per the charge and statement of task for this study, the committee offers a set of research questions to consider that align with its suggested approach for foundational cybersecurity. These are not, however, intended to supersede other agendas. This chapter offers a substantive research agenda to complement and work in tandem with the efforts toward a science of security described in Chapter 1. It includes a set of foundational technical problems, an outline of a set of questions that research in the social and behavioral sciences could address, and notes on cross-cutting topics, including metrics, assessments of criticality, and evaluation. A brief overview of other recent research agendas is available in Appendix C.

The committee outlines a foundationally oriented technical research agenda clustered around three broad themes that correspond to those in the strategic plan: detect (detection and attribution of attacks and vulnerabilities), protect (defensible systems that are prepared for and can resist attacks), and adapt (resilient systems that can recover from or cope with a wide range of adversarial behavior). Many familiar technical topics fall within these clusters. Of course, many challenges span these themes, and understanding how they interact with each other (for instance, protect systems with a design that supports both protection and adaptation) is important.

ATTACK DETECTION AND ATTRIBUTION

The original concept of intrusion detection, as put forth by J.P. Anderson in the 1970s[3] and further advanced by Dorothy Denning in the 1980s,[4] was to examine activity in the context of a computer system with the intent of detecting deviations from the norm that indicated malice or attack. The government invested significant resources in "intrusion-detection systems" during the late 1980s and 1990s with the aim of building systems that could accomplish the objective set out by Anderson. The

---

[3] J.P. Anderson, "Computer Security Threat Monitoring and Surveillance," April 15, 1980, http://seclab.cs.ucdavis.edu/projects/history/papers/ande80.pdf.

[4] See D.E. Denning, An intrusion-detection model, *IEEE Transactions on Software Engineering* SE-13(2):222-232, 1987; and D.E. Denning and P.G. Neumann, *Requirements and Model for IDES—A Real-Time Intrusion Detection System*, SRI International, 1985, http://www.csl.sri.com/papers/9sri/.

task of detecting new or previously unseen attacks is difficult because the wide variety of activities observed in a typical computer system can lead to a high number of false positives.

While many current information technology (IT) installations incorporate commercial "intrusion-detection" systems, most of those systems operate by recognizing the signatures of previously observed attacks. New attacks that do not replicate previously seen malicious code, data, or network traffic patterns may not be detected because their activity fails to "look like an intrusion." Some high-end intrusion-detection systems are capable of characterizing the normal activity on a network and reporting deviations from "normal" with an acceptably low false-positive rate.

The challenge is to detect behavior in a system that could lead to a "bad" situation. But defining "badness" is difficult and context-sensitive and can range from reductions in availability (denial of service) to information theft to corruption of data. For one thing, bad situations can result from the inadvertent mistakes of known good actors, not just from the behavior of attackers. And, attackers can often understand the workings of systems (including intrusion-detection systems themselves) and craft their attacks so as to appear "normal enough" to evade detection. Effective intrusion detection in the future will need to encompass more than technical signature-based pattern matching and machine learning-based classifiers. It also needs to include early detection of insider misuse, denials of service, and situational anomalies at many layers of abstraction. Organizations can employ red-teaming (running attacks against themselves) to help assess their own response and detection and capabilities. An additional difficulty is that in the era of big data, the data collected to protect against intruders may grow very large, and managing that data will become its own challenge.

With the increasing prominence of cyberattacks (especially in the military, diplomatic, and political spheres), attribution will be increasingly important once attacks are detected. Attribution—identifying with an understood degree of confidence who is responsible for a cyberattack—has increasing geopolitical significance. There are both technical questions (e.g., with what confidence can attribution be done, of what sorts of activities, and how quickly?) and questions related to trust and evidence. What constitutes evidence, and how can its context (including system-state parameters) and provenance be effectively conveyed? In addition, there are questions related to how to characterize uncertainty in attribution in ways that decision makers could use.

Attribution demands both technical approaches and knowledge about adversaries and their capabilities and intentions. Moreover, attribution is used for different purposes depending on context—sometimes to serve as a deterrent and sometimes to serve as the basis for holding attackers accountable. Depending on the need, there may be different requirements for certainty, precision, and accuracy. Improving prospects for attribution and accountability is a research area that should integrate technical and social and behavioral approaches to be most effective. Given the limitations of purely technical attribution, attribution is ultimately an all-source activity—that is, knowledge from multiple domains (not all technical) is brought to bear. Although attribution based on characteristics of attacks is in part a technical problem, devising effective ways to hold attackers accountable in a military, diplomatic, or political context is more of an issue for political or behavioral science. There are challenges, for instance, around the nature of the evidence, determining what kinds of evidence are both meaningful and persuasive, and how to convey that evidence in a convincing way to those who need to know. In cases that involve public confidence in systems, national security and geopolitical factors may come into play regarding how much to disclose, making what once might have seemed an esoteric technical challenge into a vexing political problem.

Finally, transparency and sharing of information related to detected attacks and their attribution would increase the value of attack detection for the infrastructure as a whole. In addition to exploring technical means that might enable organizations to more readily share information, this also relates to social and decision sciences that could help inform how to incentivize such sharing and how to make it effective.

DEFENSIBLE DESIGN, ARCHITECTURE, AND TECHNOLOGIES

Systems need to be designed to be more defensible. Foundational research opportunities in this space range from clean-slate approaches,[5] to high-assurance computing, to secure software development, to innovations in supporting technologies such as cryptography.

Specific areas that can help improve the security of software include understanding what classes of vulnerabilities can be detected automatically; research into languages that are more secure by default; support for end-to-end security policies along with analysis, synthesis, and compiler technology for automatic derivation of implementations of those policies; improvements in secure enclaves; tools for proving the absence of classes of errors; and virtualization—as part of a security infrastructure and as a

---

[5] "Clean slate" typically refers to efforts to escape legacy constraints and see what can be accomplished using state-of-the-art modern approaches that will help us understand existing systems and their constraints as well as point the way toward systems of the future. See, for example, Defense Advanced Research Projects Agency, "Clean-slate Design of Resilient, Adaptive, Secure Hosts (CRASH)," 2015, http://opencatalog.darpa.mil/CRASH.html, or the Qubes OS team's effort to develop a security-oriented operating system, https://www.qubes-os.org/intro/.

mitigation. In addition, ever larger systems will generate ever more data, necessitating research into how to manage increasingly large volumes of data, what data to collect and log, what sorts of analytics to apply, and how to do effective analytics in close to real-time. Connecting data and analytics to operational needs would also be fruitful. Architectural concepts meriting continued investigation include resiliency, information hiding, sandboxing, monitoring and logging, internal analytics, and so on.

Cryptography is key to many aspects of secure systems and their networked connections and interactions. Specific areas that would contribute to improving foundational cybersecurity include the following: cryptographic agility and future-proofing (e.g., quantum-resistant cryptography and other replacement options), compositional cryptographic protocols, integration of the possibility of side-channel attacks in algorithm and protocol design, making assumptions more realistic, improving the prospects and performance of homomorphic encryption, estimating not just upper bounds (how hard systems are to break) but lower bounds (to provide a sense of expected longevity), and connecting proofs of cryptographic security to the actual code in verifiable ways.

Also, importantly, improvements in hardware security help make systems more defensible. Research opportunities in this space range from techniques for verification of hardware designs to the development of security-enhanced architectures that take full advantage of new hardware capabilities. Integrating hardware security efforts with efforts elsewhere in the stack, toward an end-to-end approach, can lead to improvements. But understanding interactions between hardware and other components is also important.

RESILIENCE AND ADAPTABILITY

Not all attacks can be detected, and even the most defensible systems will have vulnerabilities. Thus, deploying systems that are resilient and adaptable is important for improving cybersecurity, and, more importantly, ensuring that work can continue. Resilience is an attribute of system operations and is critical to the functioning and operation of networks and the Internet itself. Resilience needs to be assessed and viewed as a systems operational capability. It is achieved by combinations of many different system features, not only the security components. Research is needed on how to operate through cyberattacks and on what it means to operate in a degraded mode and how to develop a system such that degraded operations are valid and sufficient to meet mission needs.[6]

---

[6] For one opinion on prioritization and reducing risks of dependence, see R. Danzig, "Surviving on a Diet of Poisoned Fruit: Reducing the National Security Risks of America's Cyber Dependencies," July 21, 2014, Center for a New American Security, https://www.

Additional research opportunities include the following: designing for adaptability, recovery, and graceful fail-over; developing the ability to assess the impact of a compromise and roll back to a pre-compromise state; physical protection and/or redundancy of key hardware components against electromagnetic pulse or other physical attack; increasing the utility of logging; understanding the tension between updateable (patchable) components and immutable components; and exploring ways to improve operational security. An additional opportunity is the design of systems that incorporate sufficient redundancy or consistency checks to help withstand or detect "supply chain attacks" (both software supply chain and hardware supply chain) that are conducted (possibly by insiders) during the development or maintenance process and the problems are far from solved.[7]

A fundamental tool both for detecting attacks and recovering from them is discovering unexpected changes. One key aspect is inspectability. If something can be changed by an attacker but cannot be inspected by a defender, the defender cannot detect the change except by its effects. Even then, the defender may not be able to deduce what component was changed and needs to be fixed. Detecting the change is critical, even if the effect of the change is completely obscure. For instance, some Intel CPUs load a specific chunk of data when starting. An unexpected change in that data would be an alerting signal, as would the discovery that one of a batch of otherwise identical CPUs is loading a different chunk. This is analogous to what is done to assess software artifacts and compare hashes of them with known good hash values. Despite the attractiveness of the concept, it is an open question to find all the components in a complex system that need to be inspected, and it is not obvious how to implement a complex system in which all changeable components can be inspected.

---

cnas.org/publications/reports/surviving-on-a-diet-of-poisoned-fruit-reducing-the-national-security-risks-of-americas-cyber-dependencies.

[7] The Defense Science Board is undertaking a study on the cyber supply chain that will review DoD supply chain risk management activities and consider opportunities for improvement (see Office of the Under Secretary of Defense for Acquisition, Technology and Logistics, "Terms of Reference—Defense Science Board Task Force on Cyber Supply Chain," November 12, 2014, http://www.acq.osd.mil/dsb/tors/TOR-2014-11-12-Cyber_Supply_Chain.pdf). There is also a Defense Advanced Research Projects Agency program exploring how to eliminate counterfeit integrated circuits from the electronics supply chain (see K. Bernstein, "Integrity and Reliability of Integrated Circuits (IRIS)," Defense Advanced Research Projects Agency, http://www.darpa.mil/program/integrity-and-reliability-of-integrated-circuits, accessed September 2016).

ILLUSTRATIVE TOPICS IN THE SOCIAL, BEHAVIORAL, AND DECISION SCIENCES

Research efforts that link social and behavioral sciences and cybersecurity should be positioned to encourage advances in cybersecurity practices and outcomes. As an example of the importance of the linkage to social, behavioral, and decision sciences, the *Federal Cybersecurity Research and Development Strategic Plan*,[8] mentioned earlier, also emphasized the concept of deterrence (in addition to detection, protection, and adaptation, discussed above). In the strategic plan, key challenges for deterrence include economic, policy, and legal mechanisms, as well as technical efforts. Below are several focus areas where insights from the behavioral and social sciences could prove useful. Small examples of how these topics could connect with and inform more traditional cybersecurity topics are offered after each. These are just examples, however, not a comprehensive list.

- How individuals interact with and mentally model systems, risk, and vulnerability—implications for defaults, user interfaces, development tools, enterprise security practices.
- Work group activities, knowledge sharing, and norm setting related to cybersecurity policies and practices—implications for how enterprise security tools are designed and deployed.
- Incentives and practices in organizations; how to manage organizations to produce desired outcomes (in this case appropriate cybersecurity outcomes)—implications for how enterprise security tools are designed and deployed and which defaults are chosen and promulgated.
- Adversary assessment, attribution, interruption, deterrence, and managed engagement—implications for cyber attribution research.
- Understanding and mitigating insider threat—detecting and stopping the malicious insider remains a hard problem. Having the benefit of the best thinking from social scientists will certainly help make advances on this problem. For example, what is known about what leads to security or safety infractions not being reported, and to what extent do results from other domains apply in a cybersecurity context? Similarly, what is understood about the causes of insider betrayal (such as greed, blackmail, or revenge), and are there demonstrated ways organizations can mitigate these risks?

---

[8] National Science and Technology Council, *Federal Cybersecurity Research and Development Strategic Plan: Ensuring Prosperity and National Security*, Networking and Information Technology Research and Development Program, February 2016.

- Why and how cybersecurity measures are adopted by individuals, groups, organizations, institutions, and adversaries—implications for the design of tools and practices and for dissemination, prioritization, and implementation.
- Assessing and understanding acquisition practices, business norms, and evaluation practices when software and systems are acquired and what impacts those norms and practices have on cybersecurity requirements and outcomes.
- What effect will the emerging market for cybersecurity insurance have on outcomes? What models of insurance are most appropriate? (Options may include approaches similar to insurance for natural disasters, shared risk pools such as for climate change, occupational safety, or some other approach.)
- What makes "honeypots"—systems designed to simulate targets and act as decoy to attackers—effective?
- How can public trust in cybersecurity warnings be enhanced? For example, how has the Centers for Disease Control and Prevention maintained the credibility of its warnings, despite some false alarms, and what can be learned from that experience?[9]
- Economics of technology adoption and transition in companies and institutions and in developer communities—implications for the design of tools and practices and for prioritization. For people who do not want new or updated technology, under what conditions are new technology or practices likely to be acceptable?
- Understanding the market for zero-day exploits. Does the market rely on exclusivity? If so, what mechanisms are used to enforce it? To what extent are intermediaries at work? How could intermediaries be disrupted, discredited, co-opted, imitated, or punished?
- Cybersecurity skills gap. There is currently a shortage of well-qualified people entering the field of cybersecurity. The gap is large and growing. A long-term approach will be needed to get more students interested in pursuing careers in cybersecurity. Social scientists and educational researchers can help understand and make progress in closing this skills gap.
- Sectoral and intersectoral analyses—How can coordination be improved? What role does protecting the commons play?—implications for deployment and prioritization.

---

[9] A forthcoming report of a Workshop on Building Communication Capacity to Counter Infectious Disease Threats from the Forum on Microbial Threats considers the challenge of public trust and warnings in the public health context. For more information, see http://nationalacademies.org/hmd/Activities/PublicHealth/MicrobialThreats/2016-DEC-13.aspx.

- Managing conflicting needs and values at policy, organizational, and technical levels—implications for prioritization.
- Assessing and overcoming barriers to collaboration and effective practice—implications for deployment and adoption.
- Risk analysis—risk analyses that gather relevant data and carefully represent all stakeholders can provide guidance on how to communicate across the enterprise about appropriate expectations of system behavior and performance.
- Criticality analysis—how to decompose and assess the criticality of components or capabilities and dependencies among them in large, complex systems.

Efforts in these areas will be helpful to the cybersecurity challenge if they are connected to systems design, tooling, engineering, and deployment. It will be important to integrate research results from the areas above to ensure that, for example, organizations are more likely to implement effective practices and policies and that developer communities understand how users of tools and systems are likely to behave when confronted with options. One topic that could tie together both organizational science and the cybersecurity research community is the issue of adoption of policies and practices and understanding how major improvements are adopted. The research community has had many significant ideas over time, but only some of these have been widely adopted. How did this happen? How were these chosen and promulgated? Is, for instance, most of the improvement because of adoption by a few high-leverage organizations?[10]

Interdisciplinary work of the sort described above can also provide foundational principles of cybersecurity to help inform both research and practice. For example, a foundational discovery from social science work is that diversity in membership can sometimes improve the performance of problem-solving groups.[11] This principle reinforces the argument for including social scientists in cybersecurity projects. Another example of a foundational principle is that there is a trade-off between sharing information widely in an organization to improve performance and restricting information sharing to reduce damage if one part of the organization is

---

[10] C.E. Landwehr, D. Boneh, J.C. Mitchell, S.M. Bellovin, S. Landau, and M.E. Lesk, Privacy and cybersecurity: The next 100 years, *Proceedings of the IEEE* 100:1659-1673, 2012; C.E. Landwehr, "History of US Government Investments in Cybersecurity Research: A Personal Perspective," pp. 14-20 in *Proceedings of 2010 IEEE Symposium on Security and Privacy*, May 2010; C.E. Landwehr, "Computer Security," Tutorial paper, *International Journal on Information Security* 1(1):3-13, 2001.

[11] See, for example, S. Page, *The Difference: How the Power of Diversity Creates Better Groups, Firms, Schools, and Societies*, Princeton University Press, Princeton, N.J., 2008.

hacked. Research could be done on how best to make this trade-off, as well as on how an organization can be designed to function well in the face of local breaches of security. Another foundational principle is from the 2016 strategic plan: "Users . . . will circumvent cybersecurity practices that they perceive as irrelevant, ineffective, or overly burdensome." As noted above, interdisciplinary research on how to cope with this and produce more usable security tools and practices is needed.

CRITICALITY AND EVALUATION

Finally, there are two overarching challenges that will draw on both social, behavioral, and decision sciences research and the technical research outlined here.

One is the question of how to assess and determine the criticality of a particular capability or application in a given context. Literature regarding mission assurance and requirements engineering is relevant to criticality. The techniques of contextual inquiry, requirements modeling, and even ethnography are also appropriate to this topic. How can we determine or identify mission-critical aspects of a capability so as to better connect research results and outcomes to mission-critical applications? Put another way, what are the essential capabilities for a given mission, and what are those that could be deprecated, if needed? For instance, in some circumstances, maintaining an accurate location at all times might be essential; in others, maintaining the ability to collect and store data is essential. Those sorts of analyses and prioritizations require knowledge about the mission and its goals. Related to these issues is the question of how systems can be architected so that overall security can be improved at minimal cost. This will entail both deep technical understanding and social, behavioral, and decision science understanding, since the mission criticality of any given system is dependent on the context within which it is deployed.

Another overarching challenge is finding better ways to evaluate the results of technical research and prioritize the implementation of potentially high-impact results. The basic question of how to transition from research to practice is difficult. And, it is important to support a research community that can do advance work that is long horizon, high uncertainty, possibly non-appropriable, and potentially disruptive of current practices. Can we learn from social and organizational theory about how to drive focused change (e.g., leveraging new research results) to improve an organization's cybersecurity posture and outcomes? The challenge of technology transfer and adoption relates to markets as well; thus, expertise found in business schools and experience found in the venture capital community can also help inform priorities and emphasis. Competition has both positive and negative aspects. In some cases, breakthroughs in the research community are game-changing ideas that would, in fact, disrupt industry incumbents, forcing them to innovate at a faster pace. These incumbents might prefer to inhibit the unwanted disruption and the consequent market uncertainty. Scholars in business schools and venture capitalists can both offer perspectives on, for instance, how and why particular technologies have succeeded, as well as on how the structures and assumptions of markets and organizations affect technology adoption and penetration. In the federal acquisition context, for instance, government acquisition efforts can have effects on markets. The federal government obviously has some market power with its prime contractors and their immediate supply chain, although it is a challenge for it to be a smart customer in this regard. But it may have relatively less market influence with enterprise system vendors and open-source foundations. Research into how large organizations signal their needs, and thus influence the market, could be helpful.

Two important issues with respect to both criticality analysis and evaluation are cost and personnel. Some laudable approaches to security, such as the U.S. government's "Rainbow Series" of requirements for government systems, failed to achieve their goals.[12] This was in part due to the time and cost of constructing the assurance argument required for such systems, the lack of personnel sufficiently trained in formal methods to construct an adequate assurance argument, the limited usability of the fundamental model underlying the approach, and the lack of trained personnel who could evaluate systems that were intended to be the most secure.

---

[12] These were a series of computer security guidelines and standards published by the U.S. Department of Defense and the National Computer Security Center in the 1980s and 1990s. The most relevant here was the Trusted Computer System Evaluation Criteria, nicknamed "the Orange Book." See S. Lipner, "The Birth and Death of the Orange Book," *IEEE Annals of Computing History*, April-June 2015.

5

Institutional Opportunities to Improve Security Science

Attaining meaningful cybersecurity presents a broad societal challenge. Its complexity and the range of systems and sectors in which it is needed mean that any approaches are necessarily going to be multifaceted. Moreover, cybersecurity is a dynamic process involving human attackers who continue to adapt, and it is not possible to guarantee security. Instead, we might think in terms of mitigations and continually improving resilience in an environment of continuous attack and compromise.

The research cultures that have developed in the security community and in affiliated disciplines will increasingly need to adjust to embrace and incorporate lessons and results not just from a wider variety of disciplines, but also from practitioners, developers, and system administrators who are responsible for securing real-world operational systems. This chapter first explores opportunities to improve research practices, structural approaches that can help in interdisciplinary environments, and ways to address security science in federal research programs. A brief discussion of how to assess and evaluate research and how foundational efforts in cybersecurity research bear on mission criticality follows.

OPPORTUNITIES TO IMPROVE RESEARCH PRACTICE AND APPROACH

In 2015, the Computing Research Association (CRA) Committee on Best Practices for Hiring, Promotion and Scholarship published a best practice memo, "Incentivizing Quality and Impact: Evaluating Scholarship in Hiring, Tenure, and Promotion."[1] In it, they recommended an increased emphasis on scholarship and quality over quantity:

> Sheer numbers of publications (or derivative bibliometrics) should not be a primary basis for hiring or promotion, because this does not encourage researchers to optimize for quality or impact. Other proxy measures are similarly problematic. For example, whether program committee service indicates an individual's stature in the field depends on the conference.

That memo also urged changes in the publication culture in the field:

> Systemic changes throughout the publication culture would help to support better scholarship. With new technology and digital delivery, publishers could remove page limits for reference lists and could allow appendices for data, methods, and proofs. Editors, as appropriate, could consider longer submissions with the understanding that, in such cases, a longer review period would be likely. In addition to conferences with published proceedings, other professional gatherings (that do not publish proceedings) might be held where work-in-progress could be presented.

Although this memo was aimed at the computing research community broadly, similar challenges exist in cybersecurity research. Beyond negative impacts on scholarship and quality, incentives that reward frequent publication also end up draining time and energy from the pool of reviewers (who are themselves researchers). More generally, looking for ways to improve institutional incentives broadly is important. The CRA memo also emphasizes scientific and real-world impact, which has implications for cybersecurity research, since a focus on those impacts can help motivate researchers to do the hard work that is often required to support validity and transition to practice. This work can include prototyping, partnering, and persistence in resolving issues.

Given the dynamic and rapidly evolving nature of the cybersecurity problem, the research community itself has struggled to develop a sustained science of security. The CRA memo above suggests that computing research in general suffers from counterproductive incentives related to publication quantity and an emphasis on short-term results.[2] Of course,

---

[1] B. Friedman and F.B. Schneider, "Incentivizing Quality and Impact: Evaluating Scholarship in Hiring, Tenure, and Promotion," Computing Research Association, Washington, D.C., 2015, http://cra.org/resources/best-practice-memos/incentivizing-quality-and-impact-evaluating-scholarship-in-hiring-tenure-and-promotion/.

[2] These problems are not unique to the field of cybersecurity research. *The Economist* recently discussed challenges of replication and reproducibility in the psychological sciences: "Ultimately, therefore, the way to end the proliferation of bad science is not to nag people to behave better, or even to encourage replication, but for universities and funding

such problems are endemic across science. The incentives for program managers at funding agencies, for researchers, for journal reviewers, and for conference organizers unfortunately too often skew against the development and practice of solid science. Funding agencies are under pressure to achieve short-term results; the cybersecurity research landscape is multifaceted, making it a challenge to choose focus areas.

Academic researchers are incentivized to publish as often as possible; a secondary effect of this is the impetus to avoid longer-term efforts and infrastructure work. Another side effect of the emphasis on quantity is that the peer-review process itself becomes overloaded, making it hard to find high-quality reviewers. As the community's intellectual and oversight resources are stretched, incentives to submit rejected work to another venue without making improvements can also increase. In addition to reducing the quality of the literature, that tends to waste the time and energy of the reviewers who had provided comments.

Another challenge arises due to the nature of academic prototypes. Such tools and systems do not, understandably, focus on all of the details that would need to be addressed in a production-quality artifact, which can result in vulnerabilities. But it is important to take care that the innovation being represented in the prototype does not itself interfere with getting details right later (including details related to social and behavioral assumptions).

Transparency is another challenge in the practice of research. An effective security science demands (among other things) replication of studies in different contexts, not only to verify the results stated in already-published papers, but also to help determine in which other contexts the results hold. But in cybersecurity studies, the real-world participants may be loath to allow publication of research data, for fear of revealing intellectual property (as with testing proposed new security approaches), giving up competitive advantage, or compromising customer or employee privacy. Simply demanding openness is unlikely to succeed. If researchers are to devise ways to evaluate others' work and to perform replications, they will first have to listen carefully to real-world concerns.

Given the importance that society attaches to making progress in cybersecurity, it seems valuable to try to address these counterproductive incentives and pressures and to help put the community in a better position to make progress. There are opportunities to improve how research is conducted, reported, and evaluated. To situate research within a devel-

---

agencies to stop rewarding researchers who publish copiously over those who publish fewer, but perhaps higher-quality papers." In *The Economist*, "Incentive Malus," September 24, 2016, http://www.economist.com/news/science-and-technology/21707513-poor-scientific-methods-may-be-hereditary-incentive-malus.

oped scientific framework suggests that reports of research results would have to clearly articulate how the research builds on previous efforts: what models of attacks, defenses, and/or policies the research is meant to address; and how it is informed by existing knowledge and integrates with other disciplines. This would serve to advance security science by enabling independent evaluation and assessment of past claims and pointing the way to eventual impacts on real-world systems.

With regard to experimental methods and investigational approaches, there are opportunities for cybersecurity researchers to learn from the ways that other disciplines communicate about methodology. For instance, if a project involves human subjects, then make clear the characteristics of the subject pool from which the subjects were drawn, what the selection mechanism was, and what the pool's general demographics were.[3] Other questions to consider are the following: How are the subjects compensated for their time? What were the instructions that the subjects were given? What was the design of the study? What were the statistics used? There are well-understood ways to perform case studies and surveys when experiments are impractical or impossible. There are also observational studies using well-accepted techniques from anthropology, sociology, and psychology. In many cases, it is the documentation of steps toward consistency and collaboration that are difficult to do but essential both to the science of security and to enabling cross-disciplinary investigation. Identifying threats to the validity of the study and its results can also be helpful. In many cases, the act of having to write that kind of section can bring fresh insights to the problem and also help the reviewers and others who need to evaluate the work.

In systems research in computing, there are sometimes empirical components (e.g., the use and analysis of the behavior and performance of specific artifacts) that, although not involving human subjects, could be reported in ways that explicitly draw from the list above to better position the work in the literature and clarify—to both the original researchers and to ultimate consumers of the research—the potential impact and reproducibility of the results.

One specific action that researchers and those who evaluate research results could take would be to shift the standards and expectations for how results are presented, especially for research involving human

---

[3] Relying on collecting data through Mechanical Turk studies (in which very low paid workers click through a questionnaire or carry out tasks) may not yield high-value data. A separate issue is trials carried out on live systems by companies with or without the participation of academic researchers. Concerns about ethical and scientific integrity have been raised about some studies where customers may not know they are participating. (For example, a study Facebook conducted to examine how emotions spread on social media resulted in controversy over the ethics of experimentation on humans.)

subjects.[4] Social science disciplines have standard ways of reporting studies—the problems, constraints, data, methods, limitations, and results. Cybersecurity research involving human subjects can readily follow those conventions. Cybersecurity research in other domains can learn from these disciplines and develop comparable conventions. Lack of such structure can impede comprehension and create opportunities for errors of omission (e.g., inadequacies in describing designs, in justifying decisions, in sampling, and so on). For some types of research, structured reporting can help focus the design and conduct of the research that will eventually be reported. The committee identified the seemingly prosaic function of publication practices as the following potentially effective leverage points:

- Encourage structured abstracts[5]—structured abstracts facilitate rapid comprehension, are easier to read, facilitate effective peer review, are more easily evaluated and comprehended, and lend themselves more readily to meta-analyses.
- Encourage clear statements of the research questions and how results relate to improving the understanding or management of real-world problems.
- Encourage cybersecurity researchers to become trained in experimental research methods and in explaining how they have been used—both to benefit their own work, when appropriate, and to inform their work as reviewers and evaluators of others' work.
- Emphasize reporting on methodologies and expect that researchers make explicit any experimental and evaluation methodologies used in their work.
- Expect that results be appropriately contextualized, both within the broader scientific literature and with regard to the particular problem domain.
- Develop ways to track studies and outputs from projects that encourage researchers to take advantage of reviewer comments and suggestions even when papers are not accepted for publication.
- Expect that researchers explain what models of attacks, defenses, and/or policies a particular result is meant to address.
- Encourage replication of experiments and results.
- Encourage open publishing of data and software.

---

[4] See R. Maxion, "Structure as an Aid to Good Science," *Proceedings of the IFIP Working Group, Workshop on The Science of Cyber Security*, 2015, Bristol, U.K., http://webhost.laas.fr/TSF/IFIPWG/Workshops&Meetings/67/Workshop-regularPapers/Maxion-Bristol_012315.pdf.

[5] A structured abstract is an abstract with explicit, labeled sections (e.g., Problem, Method, Results, Data, Discussion) to allow for ease of comprehension and clarity.

- Be explicit about what criteria are used to assess scientific contributions.

There have been some efforts to emphasize more structured approaches in reporting and communications by cybersecurity researchers themselves, including organizing a workshop on this topic,[6] but there are opportunities to do more here as well. In particular, emphasizing reporting of this sort can have impact in two ways: It can, as discussed above, help buttress and elaborate the emerging science of security, and it can connect research results to outcomes in the real world.

The considerations described above are relatively standard in sciences used to dealing with human subject experiments. Although much of this might be seen as process-oriented, in the committee's view, looking for opportunities to encourage these sorts of activities in the research enterprise—on the part of both funders and researchers—can help induce increased care with respect to how problems are framed and more thoughtfulness with regard to potential impact and leverage of the eventual results. Care also needs to be taken to ensure that overly rigid criteria are not used; excessive rigidity runs the risk of excluding categories of relevant and high-quality research. The assessment process itself should be under ongoing scrutiny to prevent this.

STRUCTURAL APPROACHES TOWARD IMPROVED INTERDISCIPLINARITY

To achieve effective interdisciplinary outcomes, work will need to be done across disciplinary boundaries—incorporating experts from many disciplines as well as individuals with deep expertise in more than one discipline.[7] There are often institutional impediments related to the difficulties of interdisciplinary work—for instance, regarding the respect members of one discipline give members of other disciplines; ensuring that cultural differences across disciplines reflecting conventions for documenting studies and their results are respected; and appropriate incorpo-

---

[6] *Proceedings of the IFIP Working Goup, Workshop on The Science of Cyber Security,* 2015, Bristol, U.K.

[7] At the doctoral level, the University of Bochum in Germany is pioneering Tandem Dissertations in the SecHuman Doctoral Training Centre. A technical and a social science doctoral student and their primary advisors are paired in "tandems" and carry out research on the same topic, formulating interrelated research questions and tackling them with knowledge and methods from their background, reaching conclusions within each discipline first, and then reflecting on what emerges when they put the results together. This way, each doctoral student produces a thesis that can be examined and understood by members of their own discipline, but then also provides an additional layer of insight.

ration of each discipline's perspective in each step of the research. A recent National Research Council effort looked more broadly at the challenges of "team science" and the particular challenges of collaboration. The resulting report, *Enhancing the Effectiveness of Team Science*,[8] offers policy recommendations for science research agencies and policy makers along with recommendations for individual scientists and universities. A separate effort explored the challenge of interdisciplinary research specifically at the intersection of computing research and sustainability. That report, *Computing Research for Sustainability*, offered a number of examples[9] of opportunities to enhance interdisciplinary approaches that could also be applied to the interdisciplinary challenge in cybersecurity. A revised and extended version of those opportunities that focuses on cybersecurity research follows:

- Scholarships and fellowships both for computer science graduate students and for early-career professors that provide financial support for taking the time to develop expertise in a complementary discipline.
- The development of cross-agency initiatives that encourage interdisciplinary collaboration in relevant fields.
- Support for a regular series of workshops for graduate students and junior faculty on research methods and quality scholarship.
- Support for the development of new cross-discipline structures (perhaps departments or institutes) between cybersecurity and other fields that can create a new generation of students who are agile both in technical aspects of cybersecurity and in one of the social, behavioral, or decision sciences.
- Involvement of academic administrators and others who influence the context in which tenure and promotion decisions are made. For instance, incentives could be devised to include providing a pathway for publication in social science venues that can lead to tenure and promotion, as well as framing projects so that graduate students can be involved and use the results for doctoral dissertations.
- Community meetings and other opportunities for collaborative and informal intellectual exchange focused on improving methods and approaches separate from the publication pipeline and review process prior to publication and the review process. The National

---

[8] National Research Council, *Enhancing the Effectiveness of Team Science*, The National Academies Press, Washington, D.C., 2015.

[9] See "Programmatic and Institutional Opportunities to Enhance Computer Science for Sustainability" in National Research Council, *Computing Research for Sustainability*, The National Academies Press, Washington, D.C., 2012.

Security Agency's lablets advance this approach, and much activity at conferences is of this sort.

- Institutional structures that support multidisciplinary and interdisciplinary teams focused on a problem or set of problems over an appropriately long period of time.
- The possibility of funding and support for one or more years for individuals to work in small teams on specific topics.
- Coordination between academic research in cybersecurity and nontraditional industrial partners in sectors beyond the large information technology companies—to scope problems, help train students, and cross-fertilize ideas.
- Regular, high-level summits involving cybersecurity and social science experts—practitioners and researchers—to inform shared research design, assess progress, and identify gaps and opportunities.

Another role that funding agencies can play is to fund longer-term projects and to be tolerant of uncertainty, particularly in these multidisciplinary and cross-disciplinary, potentially high-impact research areas.

In addition to applying knowledge from other disciplines to the cybersecurity challenge, foundational cybersecurity efforts would also benefit from a deeper understanding of methods from other disciplines and how they might apply to cybersecurity. Applying methods of social, behavioral, and decision sciences in cybersecurity research, where appropriate, is a way to enhance foundational approaches and also to open up potentially fruitful areas of insight and inquiry that more traditional technically focused agendas might overlook. In the committee's view, there are fundamental research directions in the social sciences that could help increase understanding of and help solve some cybersecurity problems. However, these directions are not well explored and are typically not treated as a first-class area of research in either the social sciences or in computer science and cybersecurity research. Areas from which cybersecurity research efforts might benefit include the following:

- *Predictive models*—integrating behavioral science in formal models; elicitation of expert knowledge;
- *Failure analysis*—predicting the scope and impact of a component compromise in a large-scale system;
- *Policy analysis*—especially the role of regulation and uncertainty analysis;
- *Program evaluation*—criteria setting and standards of evidence; and
- *Communication*—for education of decision makers, researchers, and users and deployers of technologies.

ADDRESSING FOUNDATIONAL CYBERSECURITY RESEARCH IN FEDERAL PROGRAMS

The committee was asked to consider gaps in the federal research program. In the committee's view, the security community and funders understand the breadth of the challenge. The Networking and Information Technology Research and Development Program's 2016 *Federal Cybersecurity Research and Development Strategic Plan* (summarized briefly in Appendix C) lays out a broad approach to addressing it. And, as an earlier National Research Council report[10] noted, emphasizing progress on all fronts along with experimentation in terms of programmatics is still important—a diversity evident in the different approaches and strategies among the federal agencies supporting cybersecurity research. The gaps that the committee identifies are not strictly topics or problems that are not being addressed. Instead, the committee recommends shifts in approaches to how programs and projects are framed, and an emphasis on seeking evidence of connections with and integration of science of security; relevant social, behavioral, and decision sciences; and operational and life-cycle understandings.

Cybersecurity poses grand challenges that require unique collaborations among the best people in the relevant core disciplines, who typically have other options for their research. Sponsors of cybersecurity research need to create the conditions that make it worth their while to work on these issues. If successful, cybersecurity research will benefit not only from the substantive knowledge of the social, behavioral, and decision sciences, but also from absorbing their research culture, with respect to theory building, hypothesis testing, method validation, experimentation, and knowledge accumulation—just as these sciences will learn from the complementary expertise of the cybersecurity community. Thus, these collaborations have transformative potential for the participating disciplines, as well as the potential to address the urgent practical problems of cybersecurity.

The traditional decoupling of academic research from engineering, quality control, and operations leaves gaps in a domain like cybersecurity, where solutions are needed for systems deployed at scale in the real world. These gaps spotlight the importance of not just technology transfer, but of incorporating a life-cycle understanding (from development to deployment, maintenance, administration, and aftermarket activities) into proposed foundational research approaches. This incorporation can lead

---

[10] National Research Council, *Toward a Safer and More Secure Cyberspace*, The National Academies Press, Washington, D.C., 2007.

to better outcomes as well as improvements in communicating how and why certain things should be done.

Many of the technical research questions this committee highlights above are addressed in various funding portfolios and in the recent strategic plan. The committee urges an emphasis on situating research efforts in security science within the framework outlined in this report, which can help spotlight high-leverage opportunities for impact, and on thinking about how those opportunities can be translated into practice and deployed at scale. This goes beyond a traditional technology transfer challenge—which is hard enough—to connecting research results with anticipated social, behavioral, and organizational implications and with what practitioners understand about managing the full life cycle of deployed technologies.

ASSESSMENT AND EVALUATION

With regard to all of these efforts, agencies that sponsor research in cybersecurity will continue to face a significant challenge in assessing the effectiveness of their investments. In part, that is the nature of research, where the ultimate payoffs can be quite large but are usually unpredictable and often come long after the research was carried out.[11] Even so, successful technology transfer and the implementation of real-world systems or subsystems that apply research results provide some measures of research quality and effectiveness.

There are extrinsic impediments related to industry practices and norms that thwart the transition of promising research ideas into practice. For example, some industry norms and expectations can hinder the adoption of ideas and may even create counter-incentives. These norms, many of which are unique to software-based systems, relate to license

---

[11] The Computer Science and Telecommunications Board's (CSTB's) recently revised "tire tracks" diagram links government investments in academic and industry research to the ultimate creation of new information technology industries with multibillion-dollar markets. Used in presentations to Congress and executive branch decision makers and discussed broadly in the research and innovation policy communities, the tire tracks figure dispelled the assumption that the commercially successful IT industry is self-sufficient, underscoring through long incubation periods of years and even decades. The figure was updated in 2002, 2003, and 2009 reports produced by the CSTB and more recently in 2012 (National Research Council, *Continuing Innovation in Information Technology*, The National Academies Press, Washington, D.C., 2012). In 2016, the CSTB issued a summary of presentations by leading academic and industry researchers and industrial technologists describing key research and development results and their contributions and connections to new IT products and industries, illustrating these developments as overlays to the "tire tracks" graphic (National Academies of Sciences, Engineering, and Medicine, *Continuing Innovation in Information Technology: Workshop Report*, The National Academies Press, Washington, D.C., 2016).

terms (e.g., as is, no warranty, and limits on acceptance evaluation with respect to security), process compliance, anticipated risk and reward (and associated measurement difficulties), and intellectual property protection. Technical advances can help address these challenges. These norms are well established and may not evolve in ways that enhance incentives for improved security. But research leaders need to be aware of these extrinsic factors as they develop ideas and plan for potential transition into practice. And, of course, advances in the technology might possibly result in adaptation of the norms to enhance the ability to develop, evaluate, and evolve improvements in security. This space itself offers opportunities for research efforts that may reveal the interplay of these norms with the potential transition and acceptance of new technologies.

Unfortunately, technology transfer can be a process of years for some research results. Moreover, a rigid focus on traditional technology transfer could drive sponsors to support only advanced development or research that leads to incremental improvements in technology, while the current state of cybersecurity clearly calls for more extensive changes.

Thus, in addition to monitoring technology transfer of applied or incremental results, sponsors can consider the following ways of assessing research:

- Publication of research results in high-quality journals or conference proceedings is the canonical indicator of research quality. To the extent that journals or conferences include editors, reviewers, or program committee members from development organizations and from other disciplines, their selections may be an especially useful indication of the long-term value of research (see also the next point).
- Creating opportunities for and then examining results of experimental prototype deployments can be instructive. Experimentation with prototypes offers the opportunity to expose hidden assumptions about reality and to demonstrate (or fail to demonstrate) scalability and feasibility.
- Technology transfer ultimately requires that results be adopted by development organizations that build real systems, by security vendors, and by organizations and institutions that deploy systems. Many development organizations and security vendors monitor research results with the aim of identifying potentially useful ideas or techniques. Feedback on research from such organizations, either in the form of informal reactions at conferences or in response to surveys or questions by sponsors, will give the sponsors a sense of research quality. Similarly, other positive signals to look for are when technical research results explicitly take

into account the behavioral and organizational considerations that influence adoption, or when the primary focus is on social and behavioral aspects of cybersecurity practices and policies and those results are recognized within a multidisciplinary research community. It is important to note that adoption is only one signal, however, and relying too much on it may inadvertently neglect disruptive approaches (e.g., so-called clean-slate efforts) that would likely have a longer path to impact and recognition.

- To the extent that research results lead to the formation of start-up companies or the hiring of researchers by commercial enterprises, sponsors should consider that a positive sign for the research effort. However, these are steps along the way, not outcomes of better security. Citations of research results by publications and researchers that are themselves successful at technology transfer (or in descriptions of successful products) are an indication of research quality, though a "lagging indicator" that will likely be available only years after the initial research has been completed.

None of these approaches is likely to be a surprise to research funders, nor a panacea that guarantees accurate assessment of results. However, all may be worth sponsors' consideration as they evaluate their research programs and associated projects they have chosen to sponsor and researchers they have chosen to support.

MISSION CRITICALITY

The committee was also asked to consider how foundational efforts in cybersecurity bear on mission-critical applications and challenges, such as those faced by agencies in the Special Cyber Operations Research and Engineering (SCORE) interagency working group (often in classified domains). First, whatever the application in whatever domain (from protecting systems that contain information on an intelligence agency's sources and methods, to preventing the servers running the latest best-selling augmented reality mobile game from being compromised, to general deterrence efforts), the same fundamental assumptions about the nature of technological systems and about human nature apply. Thus, foundational efforts, in cybersecurity as described in this report, could yield results that are broadly applicable. Second, one significant distinction that may bear on what research problems are tackled and how well solutions apply across classified and unclassified efforts in cybersecurity involves the nature of threat and what is known and by whom about that threat. Even so, as private-sector companies and enterprises are increasingly seeking to secure themselves generally against "nation-state"-level attacks, that distinction may be less critical. Third, people and processes need to be taken into account. In classified environments whose systems need to be secured, different kinds of security training might be done and different controls in terms of configuration and processes put in place than are likely in most private-sector organizations. This could have an impact on how effective certain security approaches and tools are—but the general point that social, behavioral, and decision sciences in tandem with technical cybersecurity research can help inform better choices in terms of people, processes, and institutional policies still holds.

There are undoubtedly research efforts in the classified and unclassified domains that leverage similarities in basic technologies, the nature of humans interacting with systems, and the nature of organizations. Making those connections is not always done, however. It falls to funders, the researchers, and the consumers of research to ask for and seek out those connections. In both directions, problems and assumptions may need to be translated across the classified/unclassified boundary, but foundational results should be applicable in each. In some cases, experts in a classified environment can develop study problems and data sets that are accessible to unclassified researchers. If this is accomplished well, then results can be translated into the classified setting. It will be particularly important to find and develop people who are skilled at developing and communicating these translations.

Specific areas of inquiry that could have direct applicability to SCORE missions include attribution and defense against and recovery from attacks by insiders—progress on both would benefit from the four-pronged approached recommended here. How can investments in foundational work of the sort the committee urges here be useful to those defending and supporting our nation's most critical infrastructures and defense systems? The committee believes that increasing emphasis on a deep understanding of general classes of attacks, policies, and defenses, and carefully mapping where particular research results or technology solutions fit within that understanding, can provide decision makers a more thorough and grounded understanding of likely effectiveness for their situations. Similarly, improved integration of social, behavioral, and decision science methods, results, and inputs on particular research projects will enable a more nuanced understanding of cybersecurity challenges. And SCORE agencies are likely to benefit, especially from work that helps them understand where the leverage points for improvement are likely to be—which may not always be solely technical in nature.

* * *

The challenge of cybersecurity and the urgent nature of risks to society posed by insecure systems and a dynamic and fast-changing environment understandably promotes an emphasis on moving fast. Paradoxically, however, the field is still so comparatively new and the nature of the challenge is so hard, that in-depth scientific research is needed to understand the very nature of the artifacts in use, the nature of software, the complexity and interdependencies in these human-built systems, and importantly, how the humans and organizations who design, build, use, and attack the systems affect what can be known and understood about them. Encouraging research to address these challenges will require sustained commitments and engagements. Thus, programs that encourage long-horizon projects where these connections can be worked out will be important.

The fact that these systems are designed, developed, deployed, and used by humans, and that humans are also the adversaries behind attacks on them, means that the work done in the social, behavioral, and decision sciences will be critical. Deepening our understanding of humans and human organizations, and linking that understanding to more traditional research in cybersecurity, is necessary to develop a robust security science and to deploy systems most effectively so that they do what they were designed to do, to say nothing of securing them against human adversaries. Cybersecurity can be viewed as a cutting edge of computing that demands a broad, multidisciplinary effort. Addressing the global cybersecurity challenge needs not just computer science, engineering science, and mathematics, but also draws on what we know and understand about human nature and how humans interact with and manage systems—and each other.

Appendixes

A

Briefers to the Study Committee

Susan Alexander, IARPA
Ross Anderson, University of Cambridge
L. Jean Camp, Indiana University
Deanna Caputo, MITRE
Charles Clancy, Virginia Tech
Dave Clark, Massachusetts Institute of Technology
Jerry Davis, University of Michigan
Drew Dean, Defense Advanced Research Projects Agency
Donna Dodson, National Institute of Standards and Technology
Jeremy Epstein, National Science Foundation
Mike Fisk, Los Alamos National Laboratory
Erica Fuchs, Carnegie Mellon University
Robert Herklotz, Air Force Office of Scientific Research
Lee Holcomb, Cyber Security Research Alliance
Steve King, Department of Defense
Stuart Krohn, National Security Agency
John Manferdelli, Intel
Brad Martin, Special Cyber Operations Research and Engineering
    Interagency Working Group
Keith Marzullo, National Science Foundation
Doug Maughan, Science and Technology Directorate, Department of
    Homeland Security
Tyler Moore, Southern Methodist University
Bill Newhouse, National Institute of Standards and Technology

Edward Rhyne, Department of Homeland Security
Chuck Romine, National Institute of Standards and Technology
Angela Sasse, University College London
Sami Saydjari, Cyber Defense Agency
William Scherlis, Carnegie Mellon University
Fred Schneider, Cornell University
Howard Shrobe, Defense Advanced Research Projects Agency
Gary Tartanian, USCYBERCOM Operations
Cliff Wang, Department of Energy
Yul Williams, National Security Agency
Neal Ziring, Information Assurance Directorate, National Security Agency

B

Committee Biographies

BARUCH FISCHHOFF, *Co-Chair*, is Howard Heinz University Professor, Department of Engineering and Public Policy and the Institute for Politics and Strategy, Carnegie Mellon University. A graduate of the Detroit Public Schools, he holds a B.S. (mathematics, psychology) from Wayne State University and a Ph.D. (psychology) from the Hebrew University of Jerusalem. He is a member of the National Academy of Medicine and has served on many committees of the National Academies of Sciences, Engineering, and Medicine. He is past president of the Society for Judgment and Decision Making and of the Society for Risk Analysis. He has chaired the Food and Drug Administration Risk Communication Advisory Committee and been a member of the Eugene Commission on the Rights of Women, the Department of Homeland Security (DHS) Science and Technology Advisory Committee, and the Environmental Protection Agency Scientific Advisory Board, where he chaired the Homeland Security Advisory Committee. His books include *Acceptable Risk, Risk: A Very Short Introduction, Judgment and Decision Making, A Two-State Solution in the Middle East, Counting Civilian Casualties,* and *Communicating Risks and Benefits.* He has co-chaired three National Academies' Sackler Colloquia on the Science of Science Communication.

PETER J. WEINBERGER, *Co-Chair*, has been a software engineer at Google, Inc., since 2003, working on software infrastructure. He has a Ph.D. in mathematics (number theory) from the University of California, Berkeley (UC Berkeley). After a stint at the University of Michigan, Ann Arbor, he moved to Bell Labs. At Bell Labs, he worked on Unix and did research on various topics before moving into research management, ending up as information sciences research vice president. After AT&T and Lucent split, he moved to Renaissance Technologies, a technical trading hedge fund, as head of technology. He has been on the Army Science Board, and for the National Academies he served on the Computer Science and Telecommunications Board and participated in a number of studies, including one that produced *Asking the Right Questions about Electronic Voting* and one that produced *Bulk Collection of Signals Intelligence: Technical Options*. From 2008 to 2016, he was on the Information Security and Privacy Advisory Board, the last 2 years as chair.

JANDRIA S. ALEXANDER is principal director of the Cyber Security Subdivision, The Aerospace Corporation. Ms. Alexander has been with The Aerospace Corporation since 1992 and leads cyber and information assurance architecture definition, technology assessments, vulnerability and countermeasures experiments, cyber command and control, and security engineering and acquisition for the Department of Defense, the Intelligence Community, and civil customers. She has a B.S. in computer science from Brandeis University and an M.S. in technology management from American University.

ANNIE I. ANTÓN is a professor in and chair of the School of Interactive Computing at the Georgia Institute of Technology. She has served the national defense and intelligence communities in a number of roles since being selected for the Institute for Defense Analyses (IDA)/Defense Advanced Research Projects Agency (DARPA) Defense Science Study Group in 2005 and 2006. Her current research focuses on the specification of complete, correct behavior of software systems that must comply with federal privacy and security regulations. She is founder and director of ThePrivacyPlace.org. Dr. Antón currently serves on various boards and committees, including the following: the DHS Data Privacy and Integrity Advisory Committee, an Intel Corporation advisory board, and the Future of Privacy Forum advisory board. She is a former member of the Computing Research Association (CRA) board of directors, the National Science Foundation (NSF) Computer and Information Science and Engineering Directorate Advisory Council, the Distinguished External Advisory Board for the TRUST Research Center at UC Berkeley, the DARPA Information Science and Technology Study Group, the U.S. Association for Computing Machinery Public Council, the advisory board for the Electronic Privacy Information Center in Washington, D.C., the Georgia Tech Alumni Association board of trustees, the Microsoft Research University Relations Faculty Advisory Board, the CRA-W, and the Georgia Tech Advisory

Board. Prior to joining the faculty at Georgia Tech, she was a professor of computer science in the College of Engineering at North Carolina State University. Dr. Antón is a three-time graduate of the College of Computing at the Georgia Institute of Technology, receiving a Ph.D. in 1997 with a minor in management and public policy, an M.S. in 1992, and a B.S. in 1990 with a minor in technical and business communication.

STEVEN M. BELLOVIN is a professor of computer science at Columbia University, where he does research on networks, security, and especially why the two do not get along. During the 2012–2013 academic year, he was on leave from the university and serving as the chief technologist of the Federal Trade Commission. He joined the faculty in 2005 after many years at Bell Labs and AT&T Labs Research, where he was an AT&T fellow. He received a B.A. degree from Columbia University and an M.S. and a Ph.D. in computer science from the University of North Carolina, Chapel Hill. While a graduate student, he helped create Netnews; for this, he and the other perpetrators were given the 1995 Usenix Lifetime Achievement Award (The Flame). He is a member of the National Academy of Engineering (NAE) and is serving on DHS's Science and Technology Advisory Committee and the Technical Guidelines Development Committee of the Election Assistance Commission. He has also received the 2007 National Institute of Standards and Technology/National Security Agency (NSA) National Computer Systems Security Award. Dr. Bellovin is the coauthor of *Firewalls* and *Internet Security: Repelling the Wily Hacker* and holds a number of patents on cryptographic and network protocols. He has served on many National Academies' study committees, including those on information systems trustworthiness, the privacy implications of authentication technologies, and cybersecurity research needs; he was also a member of the information technology subcommittee of a study group on science versus terrorism. He was a member of the Internet Architecture Board from 1996 to 2002; he was co-director of the Security Area of the Internet Engineering Task Force from 2002 through 2004.

SEYMOUR E. GOODMAN is a Regents' Professor, professor of international affairs and computing, and adjunct professor of history at Georgia Tech. He also serves as a co-director of the Center for International Strategy, Technology, and Policy and was founding director and now director emeritus of the Sam Nunn Security Program (Nunn-MacArthur Program). Dr. Goodman studies international developments in the information technologies and technological innovation and its effective implementation and deployment in large-scale conflicts. He has over 150 publications and has served on many academic, government, and industry editorial, study, and advisory committees, including the Computer Science and Telecommunications Board of the National Academies. He is a lifetime national associate of the National Academy of Sciences. Prior to coming to Georgia Tech he was the director of the Consortium for Research in Information Security and Policy, with the Center for International Security and Cooperation at Stanford University. He has held a variety of appointments at the University of Virginia (Applied Mathematics, Computer Science, Soviet and East European Studies), the University of Chicago (Economics), Princeton University (The Woodrow Wilson School of Public and International Affairs, Mathematics), and the University of Arizona (MIS, Soviet and Russian Studies, Middle Eastern Studies). Dr. Goodman was an undergraduate at Columbia University and obtained his Ph.D. from the California Institute of Technology in 1970, where he worked on problems of applied mathematics and mathematical physics.

RONALD GRAHAM currently holds the Irwin and Joan Jacobs Endowed Chair in Computer and Information Science in the Computer Science and Engineering Department at the University of California, San Diego (UCSD). He is also chief scientist of the California Institute for Telecommunications and Information Technology at UCSD. He joined the UCSD faculty in 1999 after a 37-year career with AT&T. Dr. Graham received his Ph.D. in mathematics from UC Berkeley in 1962. From 1962 to 1995, he was director of information sciences at AT&T Bell Labs, and from 1996 to 1999 he was chief scientist at AT&T Labs. He has held visiting professorships at Rutgers University, Princeton University, Caltech, Stanford University, and the University of California, Los Angeles, and holds six honorary doctorates. Dr. Graham is a member of the National Academy of Sciences and has served as its treasurer for 12 years. He is a past president of the American Mathematical Society and the Mathematical Association of America. He is a fellow of the American Association of Arts and Sciences, the Society for Industrial and Applied Mathematics, the Association for Computing Machinery (ACM), and the New York Academy of Sciences. Dr. Graham has won numerous awards in the field of mathematics, including the Polya Prize in Combinatorics, the Euler Medal in Combinatorics, the Allendoerfer Award, the Ford Award, and the Steele Prize for Lifetime Achievement in Mathematics (from the American Mathematical Society).

CARL LANDWEHR is lead research scientist at the Cyber Security and Privacy Research Institute at George Washington University and an independent consultant. He received his B.S. degree in engineering and applied science from Yale University and M.S. and Ph.D. degrees in computer and communication sciences from the University of Michigan, where he helped implement the MERIT packet-switched network. From

1976 to 1999, he conducted research in what would now be called cybersecurity at the Naval Research Laboratory. From 1999 to 2001, while at Mitretek Systems, he assisted several of DARPA's Information Assurance programs. From 2001 to 2005 and again from 2009 to 2011, he headed the NSF's research programs to advance trustworthy computing, receiving the NSF Director's Award for Meritorious Service in 2012. From 2005 to 2009, he managed programs in both defensive and offensive cyber operations at I-ARPA (the Intelligence Advanced Research Projects Activity) and its predecessor organizations. He has been active in the Institute of Electrical and Electronics Engineers (IEEE), including two terms as editor-in-chief of *IEEE Security and Privacy Magazine,* in the ACM, and in International Federation for Information Processing (IFIP) Working Groups 11.3 and 10.4, and he has received a variety of awards for research and service from these organizations. He has served on several National Academies' study committees and has advised DARPA, NSA, Sandia National Laboratories, Massachusetts Institute of Technology Lincoln Laboratories, Australia's Defence Science and Technology Organisation, Israel's Council for Higher Education, and similar institutions. He has taught courses in computer science at Purdue University, Georgetown University, the University of Maryland, and Virginia Tech. In 2012, he was in the first class of 11 individuals inducted into the Cyber Security Hall of Fame. In 2015–2016, he served as Visiting McDevitt Professor of Computer Science at LeMoyne College, where he developed and taught a new course, "Cybersecurity for Future Presidents." In 2016, he was elected to the board of directors of the nonprofit Center for Democracy and Technology.

STEVEN B. LIPNER is executive director of SAFECode, a nonprofit organization dedicated to increasing trust in information and communications technology products and services through the advancement of effective software assurance methods. He retired in 2015 as partner director of software security in Trustworthy Computing at Microsoft Corporation. His expertise is in software security, software vulnerabilities, Internet security, and organization change for security. He is the founder and long-time leader of the Security Development Lifecycle (SDL) team that has delivered processes, tools, and associated guidance and oversight that have significantly improved the security of Microsoft's software. Mr. Lipner has over 40 years of experience as a researcher, development manager, and general manager in information technology security. He served as executive vice president and general manager for Network Security Products at Trusted Information Systems and has been responsible for the development of mathematical models of security and of a number of secure operating systems. Mr. Lipner was one of the initial 12 members of the U.S. Computer Systems Security and Privacy Advisory Board (now the Information Security and Privacy Advisory Board) and served two terms and a total of 10 years on the board. He is the author of numerous professional papers and has spoken on security topics at many professional conferences. He is named as inventor on 12 U.S. patents in the fields of computer and network security and has served on numerous scientific boards and advisory committees, including as a current member of the National Academies' Committee on Future Research Goals and Directions for Foundational Science in Cybersecurity and the Committee on Law Enforcement and Intelligence Access to Plaintext Information in an Era of Widespread Strong Encryption: Options and Tradeoffs. Mr. Lipner was elected in 2015 to the National Cybersecurity Hall of Fame and in 2017 to the National Academy of Engineering.

ROY MAXION is a research professor in the Computer Science, Machine Learning and Electrical and Computer Engineering Departments at Carnegie Mellon University (CMU), and director of the CMU Dependable Systems Laboratory. His general research interests are rooted in system dependability and reliability, recently turning toward information assurance, behavioral biometrics, and selected aspects of computer security. He has been program chair of the International Conference on Dependable Systems and Networks and a member of the executive board of the IEEE Technical Committee on Fault Tolerance, the U.S. Defense Science Board, and various professional organizations. He has consulted for the U.S. Department of State as well as for numerous industry and government bodies. He is presently on the editorial boards of the *International Journal of Biometrics* and *IEEE Security and Privacy* and is past associate editor of *IEEE Transactions on Dependable and Secure Computing*, the *IEEE Transactions on Information Forensics and Security*, and *International Journal of Security and Networks*. He is an elected member of the IFIP Working Group 10.4 on Dependable Systems. Dr. Maxion is a fellow of the IEEE.

GREG MORRISETT is the dean of Computing and Information Sciences (CIS) at Cornell University, which houses the departments of Computer Science, Information Science, and Statistical Sciences. From 2004 to 2015, he held the Allen B. Cutting Chair in Computer Science at Harvard University. At Harvard, he also served as the associate dean for Computer Science and Electrical Engineering and as the director of the Center for Research on Computation and Society. Before Harvard, Dr. Morrisett spent 8 years on the faculty of Cornell's Computer Science Department. He received his bachelor's degree from the University of Richmond and both his master's and doctorate degrees from CMU. His research focuses on the application of programming language technology for building secure, reliable, and high-performance software systems. A common theme is the focus on systems-level languages and tools that can help detect or prevent common vulnerabilities in software. Past examples include typed assembly language, proof-carrying code, software fault isolation, and control-flow isolation. Recently, his research focuses on building provably correct and secure software, including a focus on cryptographic schemes, machine learning, and compilers. Dr. Morrisett is a fellow of the ACM and has received a number of awards for his research on programming languages, type systems, and software security, including a Presidential Early Career Award for Scientists and Engineers, an IBM Faculty Fellowship, an NSF Career Award, and an Alfred P. Sloan Fellowship. He served as chief editor for the *Journal of Functional Programming* and as an associate editor for *ACM Transactions on Programming Languages and Systems, Information Processing Letters*, and *The Journal of the ACM*. He currently serves as co-editor-in-chief for the Research Highlights column of Communications of the ACM. In addition, Dr. Morrisett has served on the DARPA Information Science and Technology Study Group, the NSF Computer and Information Science and Engineering Advisory Council, The Max Planck Institute for Software Systems Advisory Board, the CRA board, Microsoft Research's Technical Advisory Board, Microsoft's Trustworthy Computing Academic Advisory Board, and the Fortify Technical Advisory Board.

BRIAN SNOW is an independent security advisor. As a mathematician/ computer scientist, Mr. Snow taught mathematics and helped lay the groundwork for a computer science department at Ohio University in the late 1960s. He joined the NSA in 1971, where he became a cryptologic designer and security systems architect. Dr. Snow spent his first 20 years at the NSA doing and directing research that developed cryptographic components and secure systems. Many cryptographic systems serving the U.S. government and military use his algorithms; they provide capabilities not previously available and span a range from nuclear command and control to tactical radios for the battlefield. Computer security, network security, and strong assurance were major aspects for these systems. He created and managed the NSA's Secure Systems Design division in the 1980s. He has many patents, awards, and honors attesting to his creativity. His later years at the NSA were the model for what it means to be a senior technical director at the NSA (similar to a chief scientist or senior technical fellow in industry); he served in that capacity in three major mission components: the Research Directorate (1994-1995), the Information Assurance Directorate (1996-2002), and the Directorate for Education and Training—the NSA's Corporate University (2003-2006). He was the first technical director appointed at the "Key Component" level at the NSA, and the only "techie" at the NSA to serve in such a role across three different directorates. Throughout those years, his credo was as follows: "Managers are responsible for doing things right; technical directors are responsible for finding the right things to do." In all of his positions, he insisted that the actions the NSA took to provide intelligence for our national and military leaders should not put U.S. persons or their rights at risk. He was a leading voice for always assessing the unintended consequences of both success and failure prior to taking action. Mr. Snow retired in 2006 and is now a security consultant and ethics advisor. He received his B.S. and M.S. in mathematics from the University of Colorado in 1965 and 1967, respectively, and did additional graduate course work in computer science at Ohio University from 1969 to 1971 and in mathematics at the University of Maryland from 1972 to 1973.

PHILIP VENABLES is the chief operational risk officer at Goldman Sachs. He is a member of the Firmwide Risk Committee. Previously, Mr. Venables served as chief information risk officer and head of technology risk. He joined Goldman Sachs as a vice president in London in 2000 and transferred to New York in 2001. Mr. Venables was named managing director in 2003 and partner in 2010. Prior to joining the firm, he was chief information security officer at Deutsche Bank and also functioned as the global head of technology risk management for Standard Chartered Bank. Before that, Mr. Venables served in various technology, network management, and software engineering roles at a number of finance, energy, and defense organizations. He serves on the executive committee of the U.S. Financial Services Sector Coordinating Council for Critical Infrastructure Protection and is a member of the boards of the Center for Internet Security and the New York University Tandon School of Engineering. He is also an advisor to the IDA and a U.S. intelligence agency. Mr. Venables is a member of the Council on Foreign Relations. He earned a B.Sc. (Hons.) in computer science from the University of York and an M.Sc. in computation from Queen's College at Oxford University. He was awarded the designation of chartered engineer in 1995 and chartered scientist in 2002 and was elected a fellow of the British Computer Society in 2005.

STEVEN WALLACH was a founder of Convey Computer. Micron Technology bought Convey in 2015. At Micron, Mr. Wallach is a design-engineering director. Previously, he served as vice president of technology for Chiaro Networks, Ltd., and as co-founder, chief technology officer, and senior vice president of development of Convex Computer Corporation. After Hewlett-Packard Co. (HP) bought Convex, Mr. Wallach became chief technology officer of HP's Enterprise Systems Group. He served as a consultant to the U.S. Department of Energy's Advanced Simulation and Computing Program at Los Alamos National Laboratory from 1998 to

2007. He was also a visiting professor at Rice University in 1998 and 1999, and was manager of advanced development for Data General Corporation. His efforts on the MV/8000 are chronicled in Tracy Kidder's Pulitzer Prize-winning book, *The Soul of a New Machine*. Mr. Wallach, who has 39 patents, is a member of the National Academy of Engineering, an IEEE fellow, and a founding member of the Presidential Information Technology Advisory Committee. He is the 2008 recipient of IEEE's Seymour Cray Award and the 2002 Charles Babbage award.

C

Highlights from Other Research Agendas

Computers at Risk: Safe Computing in the Information Age **(1991)**

National Research Council, National Academy Press, Washington, D.C.

The System Security Study Committee was charged with developing a national research, engineering, and policy agenda to help the United States achieve a more trustworthy computing technology base by the end of the century. In order to advance an end-to-end systems approach, this report committee also brought together two groups that did not interact much before: communications security (COMSEC) and computer security (COMPUSEC).

The committee delivered a total of six recommendations: (1) promulgate comprehensive generally accepted system security principles, (2) take specific short-term actions that build on readily available capabilities, (3) gather information and provide education, (4) clarify export control criteria and set up a forum for arbitration, (5) fund and pursue needed research, and (6) establish an information security foundation. Under the fifth recommendation, the committee highlighted a security research agenda that would include research regarding the following: (1) security modularity, (2) security policy models, (3) cost/benefit models for security, (4) new security mechanisms, (5) increasing effectiveness of assurance techniques, and (6) alternative representations and presentations. This list was not meant to be complete, but illustrated the importance and scope of a possible research agenda moving forward.

The committee highlighted that progress was needed at many fronts, including management, deployment, research, legal enforcement, and institutional support, and that the reliability of computers and communications would be essential to the United States taking advantage of the Information Age.

Trust in Cyberspace (1999)

National Research Council, National Academy Press, Washington, D.C.

The Committee on Information Systems Trustworthiness was convened to assess the nature of information systems trustworthiness and prospects for technology that will increase trustworthiness. Part of its task statement was to "propose a research agenda that identifies ideas for relevant long-term research and the promotion of fundamental or revolutionary (as opposed to incremental) advances to foster increased trustworthiness of networked information systems."

The central recommendations it made concerned the agenda for research. These recommendations included the following: (1) research to identify and understand networked information systems vulnerabilities, (2) research in avoiding design and implementation errors, (3) new approaches to computer and communication security, and (4) research in building trustworthy systems from untrustworthy components. These recommendations were aimed at federal funders of relevant researchers, such as the Defense Advanced Research Projects Agency (DARPA) and the National Security Agency (NSA), while also highlighting that policy makers should take interest in the research agenda as they formulate legislation. The committee believed that increased funding was warranted for both DARPA and the NSA for information security research and networked information systems trustworthiness research in general.

In addition to the central recommendations relating to the research agenda, the committee highlighted a number of findings and recommendations related to security and trustworthiness (Box C.1).

Embedded, Everywhere:
A Research Agenda for Networked Systems
of Embedded Computers (2001)

National Research Council, The National Academies Press, Washington, D.C.

The Committee on Networked Systems of Embedded Computers was convened to conduct a study of networked systems of embedded computers (EmNets) and examine the kinds of systems that might be developed and deployed in the future and identify areas in need of greater

BOX C.1
Findings and Recommendations from
Trust in Cyberspace **Related to Security and Trustworthiness**

The design of trustworthy networked information systems presents profound challenges for system architecture and project planning. Little is understood, and this lack of understanding ultimately compromises trustworthiness. (p. 244)

Security research during the past few decades has been based on formal policy models that focus on protecting information from unauthorized access by specifying which users should have access to data or other system objects. It is time to challenge this paradigm of "absolute security" and move toward a model built on three axioms of insecurity: insecurity exists; insecurity cannot be destroyed; and insecurity can be moved around. (p. 247)

Improved trustworthiness may be achieved by the careful organization of untrustworthy components. There are a number of promising ideas, but few have been vigorously pursued. "Trustworthiness from untrustworthy components" is a research area that deserves greater attention. (p. 251)

Imperfect information creates a disincentive to invest in trustworthiness for both consumers and producers, leading to a market failure. Initiatives to mitigate this problem are needed. (p. 251)

Consumer and producer costs for trustworthiness are difficult to assess. An improved understanding, better models, and more and accurate data are needed. (p. 252)

As a truly multidimensional concept, trustworthiness is dependent on all of its dimensions. However, in some sense, the problems of security are more challenging and therefore deserve special attention. (p. 252)

SOURCE: National Research Council, *Trust in Cyberspace*, 1999, National Academy Press, Washington, D.C.

investigation. The overall objective was to develop a research agenda that could guide federal programs related to computing research and inform the research communities (in industry, universities, and government) about the challenging needs of the emerging research area. The committee found eight key areas in which concerted research efforts were needed: predictability and manageability; adaptive self-configuration; monitoring and system health; computational models; network geometry; interoperability; the integration of technical, social, ethical, and public policy issues; and enabling technologies.

For embedded computers, the committee noted that the users of networked systems were going to demand reliability, safety, security, privacy, and ease of use—all of which were bundled together in the term "trustworthiness." Given the amount of information that can be gathered by these systems, the committee highlighted that there needed to be ways that information could be verified to ensure that it was not compromised, misused, or accessed by an outsider. The committee noted that security in the context of embedded networks needs to assume that an adversary will actively try to abuse, break, or steal from the system. It also highlighted that security analysis in embedded systems would be difficult because embedded networks expand the number of possible points of failure, tampering, or attack and homogenous embedded networks would need different security than heterogeneous embedded networks. For example, traditional network security techniques will suffice along with policy and protection methods in homogeneous embedded networks, but heterogeneous embedded networks will rely more heavily on trust management and security policies/methods at individual nodes and applications. Creating boundaries for these systems would be a problem, just taking into account their size and span as noted earlier, in addition to potential vulnerabilities that could be found in remote updates or mobile code. These boundaries would also protect these systems from denial-of-service attacks that may pose challenges to high-integrity networks, such as those found in the military.

In order to address some of the security issues noted above, the committee highlighted a few research topics that it believed could use more attention to improve the overall trustworthiness of a system, including the following:

- Fault models and recovery techniques for embedded networks that take into account their scale, long life, open architecture, distributed control aspects, and the replaceabiity of their components (Reliability)
- Embedded network monitoring and performance-checking facilities (Reliability)
- Verification of embedded networks' correctness and reliability (Reliability)
- Designing embedded networks with safety incorporated into the design, including the human–computer interface and interaction (Safety)
- Hazard analysis for embedded networks (Safety)
- Validating requirements (Safety)
- Verifying safety (Safety)
- Ensuring safety in upgraded software (Safety)

- Network access control (Security)
- Enforcement of security policies (Security)
- Critical infrastructure self-defense (Security)
- Preventing denial-of-service attacks (Security)
- Energy scarcity (which can significantly challenge security) (Security)
- Flexible policy management (Privacy)
- Informed consent (Privacy)
- Accountability research (Privacy)
- Anonymity-preserving systems (Privacy)
- Design for users and interaction (Usability)
- Appropriate conceptual models (Usability)

Toward a Safer and More Secure Cyberspace (2007)

National Research Council, The National Academies Press, Washington, D.C.

The Committee on Improving Cybersecurity Research in the United States was charged with developing a strategy for cybersecurity research in the 21st century. The committee built upon a number of previous Computer Science and Telecommunications Board reports. The committee's action agenda for policy makers had five elements. The first was to create a sense of urgency about the cybersecurity problem, as the cybersecurity policy failure is not so much one of awareness as of action. The second, commensurate with a rapidly growing cybersecurity threat, was to support a broad, robust, and sustained research agenda at levels which ensure that a large fraction of good ideas for cybersecurity research could be explored. The third was to establish a mechanism for continuing follow-up on a research agenda that would provide a coordinated picture of the government's cybersecurity research activities across the entire federal government, including both classified and unclassified research. The fourth was to support research infrastructure, recognizing that such infrastructure is a critical enabler for allowing research results to be implemented in actual information technology products and services. The fifth was to sustain and grow the human resource base, which will be a critical element in ensuring a robust research agenda in the future.

In regards to highlighting the necessities in research, the committee identified five principles that should shape the research agenda: (1) Conduct cybersecurity research as though its application will be important, (2) Hedge against uncertainty in the nature of the future threat, (3) Ensure programmatic continuity in the research agenda, (4) Respect the need for breadth in the research agenda, and (5) Disseminate new knowledge and artifacts.

The committee highlighted that there is no silver bullet for "fixing" cybersecurity, as cybersecurity will continue to grow and evolve. This means that gaining ground will require broad and ongoing society-wide efforts that focus on cybersecurity vulnerability. It also noted that earlier reports had identified research investments in a number of important areas consistent with the recommendations reiterated in its report. It clearly stated that cybersecurity needs to be made a priority by society so that research could be moved forward.

Science of Cyber-Security (2010)

JSR-10-102, JASON, The MITRE Corporation, McLean, Virginia

JASON was tasked by the Department of Defense (DoD) to perform a study on the interplay of science with cybersecurity. As a part of the study, DoD posed a number of questions to be answered by JASON, including the following:

- What elements of scientific theory, experimentation, and/or practice should the cyber security research community adopt to make significant progress in the field? How will this benefit the community? Are there philosophical underpinnings of science that the cybersecurity research community should adopt?
- Are there "laws of nature" in cyberspace that can form the basis of scientific inquiry in the field of cyber security? Are there mathematical abstractions or theoretical constructs that should be considered?
- Are there metrics that can be used to measure with repeatable results the cyber security status of a system, of a network, of a mission? Can measurement theory or practice be expanded to improve our ability to quantify cyber security?
- How should a scientific basis for cyber security research be organized? Are the traditional domains of experimental and theoretical inquiry valid in cyber security? Are there analytic and methodological approaches that can help? What are they?
- Are there traditional scientific domains and methods such as complexity theory, physics, theory of dynamical systems, network topology, formal methods, mathematics, social sciences, etc., that can contribute to a science of cyber security?
- How can modeling and simulation methods contribute to a science of cyber security?
- Repeatable cyber experiments are possible in small closed and controlled conditions, but can they be scaled up to produce repeat-

able results on the entire Internet? To the subset of the Internet that supports DoD and the Intelligence Community?

- What steps are recommended to develop and nurture scientific inquiry into forming a science of cyber security field? What is needed to establish the cyber security science community?
- Is there reason to believe the above goals are, in principle, not achievable, and if so, why not?

JASON acknowledged that the challenge in defining a science of cybersecurity is that it is an "artificially constructed environment" that does not have strong ties to the physical realm and the challenges created from this environment dynamic in nature. They highlighted that there is not one area of science that covers all the issues related to cybersecurity; however, they found other fields that they believed were analogous to cybersecurity, such as epidemiology, economics, and clinical medicine. They noted that there were specific subfields in computer science that were especially relevant to examine as well, including model checking, cryptography, randomization, type theory, and game theory. They stated that model checking could provide frameworks for examining security issues; cryptography could provide useful lessons relating to communication in the presence of an adversary and the capabilities adversaries are assumed to have; randomization or use of obfuscation could help to construct defenses; and game theory could help to prioritize cyber defense activities. In addition, they noted that machine learning and event processing would be subfields of importance when trying to correlate anomalies in systems to actual attacks.

JASON reported that although there had been a lot of reports on the need for R&D for cybersecurity, there was a universal agreement that more work was needed and that there was no agreement that it was being managed well. To move forward, one key observation by JASON was the need to accelerate the process of turning research results into tools that can be used by developers. To make significant progress in the field of cybersecurity, JASON highlighted that the most important first steps should be the creation of a common language and basic concepts that the cybersecurity community can use as a foundation, while also understanding that adversaries, threats, and practices will change over time since there are no intrinsic "laws of nature" for cybersecurity as there are in other scientific fields.

In addition to contributing their own conclusions and recommendations, JASON endorsed the IDA report *Cyber-Security Technology Initiatives*, which had recommended the establishment of cybersecurity science-based centers and projects within universities and other centers. JASON highlighted the following advantages of having DoD sponsor those programs:

1. The DoD would have access to the best ideas and people.
2. The DoD would be able to "bias the work towards their versions of common problems."
3. Universities and other research centers would be able to leverage resources internal to the DoD (including internal networks).

They also highlighted that universities and centers would be able to bridge the gap between the DoD and the software industry in order to accelerate the transition of new ideas into useful tools for developers.

Federal Cybersecurity Research and Development Strategic Plan (2016)
Executive Office of the President, Washington, D.C.

The *Federal Cybersecurity Research and Development Strategic Plan* released in February 2016 expands on the strategic plan *Trustworthy Cyberspace: Strategic Plan for the Federal Cybersecurity Research and Development Program* released in December 2011. The strategic plan is built upon four assumptions related to adversaries, defenders, users, and technology (Box C.2) and expands on the priorities set in 2011. The strategic plan also introduces a heavy focus on research and development not discussed in the 2011 strategic plan.

The strategic plan uses the four fundamental assumptions to outline near-term, mid-term, and long-term goals that together will pro-

---

BOX C.2
Four Assumptions upon Which the Plan Is Founded

Adversaries. Adversaries will perform malicious cyber activities as long as they perceive that the potential results outweigh the likely effort and possible consequences for themselves.

Defenders. Defenders must thwart malicious cyber activities on increasingly valuable and critical systems with limited resources and despite evolving technologies and threat scenarios.

Users. Users—legitimate individuals and enterprises—will circumvent cybersecurity practices that they perceive as irrelevant, ineffective, inefficient, or overly burdensome.

Technology. As technology cross-connects the physical and cyber worlds, the risks as well as the benefits of the two worlds are interconnected.

vide the tools needed to improve cybersecurity. These goals include the following:

- Near-term goal (1-3 years): Achieve S&T advances to counter adversaries' asymmetrical advantages with effective and efficient risk management.
- Mid-term goal (3-7 years): Achieve S&T advances to reverse adversaries' asymmetrical advantages through sustainably secure systems development and operation.
- Long-term goal (7-15 years): Achieve S&T advances for effective and efficient deterrence of malicious cyber activities via denial of results and likely attribution.

In order to achieve these goals, the plan focuses on developing science and technology to support what the report identifies as four defensive elements. The four defensive elements are as follows: deter, protect, detect, and adapt. The plan wants to deter malicious attacks by measuring and increasing the costs to adversaries carrying out such activities, diminishing the spoils, and increasing risks and uncertainty for potential adversaries. The plan wants components, systems, users, and critical infrastructure to have the ability to efficiently resist malicious cyber activities while also ensuring confidentiality, integrity, availability, and accountability. The plan wants the ability to efficiently detect, or even anticipate, adversary decisions based on the assumption that systems should be assumed to be vulnerable since perfect security is not possible. The plan wants defenders, defenses, and infrastructure to dynamically adapt to malicious cyber activities by efficiently reacting to disruption, recovering from damage, maintaining operations while completing restoration, and adjusting to thwart similar future activity.

The four defensive elements, which ultimately support the overall plan, are dependent on six areas deemed critical to a successful cybersecurity R&D effort: (1) scientific foundations, (2) enhancements in risk management, (3) human aspects, (4) transitioning successful research into pervasive use, (5) workforce development, and (6) enhancing the infrastructure for research.

The plan highlighted five recommendations for the federal government that would help support and achieve the plan in its entirety:

- **Recommendation 1.** Prioritize basic and long-term research in federal cybersecurity R&D.
- **Recommendation 2.** Lower barriers and strengthen incentives for public and private organizations that would broaden participation in cybersecurity R&D.

- **Recommendation 3.** Assess barriers and identify incentives that could accelerate the transition of evidence-validated effective and efficient cybersecurity research results into adopted technologies, especially for emerging technologies and threats.
- **Recommendation 4.** Expand the diversity of expertise in the cybersecurity research community.
- **Recommendation 5.** Expand diversity in the cybersecurity workplace.